FITBIZ

SECRETS OF A SEVEN-FIGURE GYM

by Daniel Nyiri

FITBIZ

Secrets Of A 7-Figure Gym

published by 4U Publishing, 2017

ISBN: 978-0-9987017-0-7

Written by Daniel Nyiri

Foreword by Topher Morrison

Cover Design by YMMY Marketing

Interior Layout Design by YMMY Marketing

Printed in the United States of America

THANK YOU:————————————

Thank you to my wife for the sleepless nights I caused when I woke up in the middle of the night to scribble down things after dreaming of an idea. Without my best friend, Greg Gutshall, this would have not been possible, since he was the one who introduced me to my amazing wife, Nina Nyiri.

Thank you for my amazing team Jessica West, Parita Patel, Ryan Oltz, Richard Storey, Grant Wiles, Erin Stern, Michael Angelo Munoz, Leandro Gongora and many, many more!

Thank you Mark Wester, for all the support, coaching, and everyday check-in. You are like a father to me, and thank you for making me a part of your amazing family.

Thank you to some of the mentors I have had in my life, especially Topher Morrison and Patrick Bet-David. Please keep doing what you are doing. You guys are amazing.

Thank you to my dear friend, Mate Varga, who believed in me when I didn't even speak English yet, and to Erin Stern, who believed enough in our brand to represent it.

A very big thanks to Mike Arce CEO of Loud Rumor, whose amazing company fuels our success and we keep competing on our success.

Speaking of competing, thanks to Lauren Davenport for being my competition in writing and finishing up this book which, let me remind you, on 1/25/17, I beat you to it. I look forward to your amazing success and I look forward to competing with you for the rest of my life in success and growth.

Of course, all this would have been impossible without my mother pulling me back down to earth and keeping my ego in check.

Finally, thanks to my father who showed me what is hardship and that nothing is given in this world; you have to work for it.

DEDICATION: ──────────────

This book is dedicated to all gym owners and personal trainers who are in this business specifically to help people, and help put a dent in the obesity crisis while making money by doing something they truly love. It is dedicated to all those trainers and owners who have given their lives to help people attain the results they have wanted, desired, and most importantly, needed. And finally, it is dedicated to those trainers and owners who are heroes that have made their lives a part of something much bigger than themselves.

To all my amazing employees, I am amazed by the talented and motivated people who are a part of our team. I am so excited and I cannot wait to have hundreds and eventually thousands of people working with us on revolutionizing the fitness industry to make an impact and eventually end obesity all together!

CONTENTS

Dedication...5

Foreword By Topher Morrison...........................11

Introduction...15

Chapter 1: Key Mistakes That Gym Owners Make...........21

Chapter 2: Get The Scale Out..........................25

Chapter 3: Welcome Your Competition
With Open Arms..29

Chapter 4: What Is Your Goal?.........................33

Chapter 5: Why Do Clients Leave?......................37

Chapter 6: Work Hard, But Don't Work All The Time.......39

Chapter 7: Work Out Your Brain.......................45

Chapter 8: What Is Your Niche?.......................49

Chapter 9: Wind Up For A Serious Pitch................55

Chapter 10: Get The Word Out.........................61

Chapter 11: Offer A Five-Star Experience..............73

Chapter 12: Nutrition Is Just As Important As Exercise......81

Chapter 13: Mind Over Matter.........................85

Chapter 14: Make The Right Hiring Decisions............91

Chapter 15: Managing A Successful Personal Training
Business...109

Chapter 16: Stay On Top Of Your Financials.............113

Chapter 17: Sell, Sell, Sell..........................115

Chapter 18: Keep 'Em Coming Back For More............121

Chapter 19: Putting It All Together...................131

Chapter 20: Feed Your Brain..........................143

Conclusion...149

Bonus Interviews.....................................153

Recommended Reading.................................162

About The Author....................................169

FOREWORD: ————————————————

By Topher Morrison
Founder at Topher Communications

"Do what you love and the money will follow." These famous words have been the source behind a countless number of people quitting their day job as a mortgage broker, financial analyst, electrician, and a host of other jobs in order to become a personal trainer. I could say the same for many other professions as well - professions that people have, at one point benefited from and thought to themselves, "How lucky are they? They get paid to do something they love!!" And, Bam! Another entrepreneur is born.

This concept of doing what you love, and having the money follow is also the source of a very similar number of people going flat broke in their new endeavor. It is quite possibly, the biggest lie ever told about entrepreneurship. I'm not saying to do something that you don't love, but simply having a passion for something isn't enough to make the money follow. You've got to run your business like — well, an actual business!

I think the part of said advice that gets people stuck in a business that isn't scalable, stresses them out financially, and consumes way too many hours in their lives, are the words "do" and "what." They imply that as a business owner you should be focused on the day to day functions of what a business does instead of focusing on running a business that you love and hiring people to do the day to day functional processes.

Daniel gets the concept of what ownership of a business is all about. He understands the difference between a functional position in the company and a vital role in the company. The more functional roles you fulfill in your business, the slower that business will grow. If all you are is functional, the business will in fact, decline. Successful business owners spend the majority, if not all of their time in vital roles in the business. What's the difference?

Functional roles are things anyone can do. If you can hire someone to do it, it's probably functional. Take a personal training studio. Cleaning the floors, re-stacking the weights, training the clients, balancing the books - all these things can be done by employees. But establishing policies and procedures for what a clean studio looks like, hiring the personal trainers and keeping them motivated, auditing the accounts receivables and payables are things that as a small business owner, you and only you should be doing. As your small business grows into a mid-sized business, even these roles can become functional and you can hire others as you become a brand ambassador and spend your energy on company vision, mission, and values.

As a business evolves, so too do the roles of what are functional and vital. If you are reading this book, then you are ready to take what may have been vital in the past, and have it become functional, so you can focus on new duties in your business that will build it and scale.

This is where it gets exciting. Remember that whole thing about doing what you love and letting the money follow? This is where the most important part of that phrase comes into play. The "love." If you take a moment to pause, and ask yourself what it is that you really love about your business. It's not the what. It's the effect of the what. The reason you are in the business you are in, I would predict, is because of the way it makes you feel when your customers benefit from what you do.

Focus on that! Because when you focus on how your clients feel as a result of what you do, that is where you can find the motivation and the discipline to grow your business way beyond what you as one person can do alone, and when you can scale what you do so that 5, 10, or even a hundred people can duplicate your what, you get to serve the world at a much greater capacity and that is when the money follows doing what you love.

In fact, this book is really about love. It's about giving you the tools to fulfill your mission in your business at a scale far greater than perhaps you even felt was possible. When you can do that, yes the money will follow, but even more importantly, the love of why you do what you do in the first place will be fulfilled beyond your dreams.

Topher Morrison

INTRODUCTION: ————————————————

"The only person you are destined to become is the person you decide to be.."

Ralph Waldo Emerson

If you own a personal training studio or a gym or you are thinking about getting into the business, this book is designed just for you! While some people think that small businesses are tough to run or destined to fail, that is not true. Ultimately, it's not the business, it's the person who owns it that will determine whether it succeeds or fails. Through my research and my own experience, I learned that personal trainers who open their own studio work even harder than personal trainers who works for a gym —and make about the same amount.

Which is not a problem. Because you do have to work. The key is to work on the right things – this means working on your business as the owner and in your business as a personal trainer. This book will show you how to work on instead of in your business! It will provide you with the right tools to implement into your business and show you how to be a great business owner. First, you must understand that a personal trainer is not a gym owner! As soon as you became a gym owner, you are entering into a new field with new roles and titles.

There are more than 36,000 gyms and studios in the United States[1]. That is an average of about 12 fitness studios per county. These fitness gyms and studios open up and close down every month. At the end of

---

1 LLC, F. H. (2017). Fitness industry analysis 2017 - cost & trends. Retrieved January 27, 2017, from https://www.franchisehelp.com/industry-reports/fitness-industry-report/

the first year, about 50% of the small independent studios shut down for good and the ones that do make it are not much better off. The average gym's revenue in the United States is less than $300,000 per year, according to the Association of Fitness Studios. The average earnings before taxes, interest and depreciation is actually $78,086, and it's even less for smaller studios. The number one studio in the United States is LA Fitness with earnings of $1.85 billion.

There are 30 million registered companies in the U.S and 96% of them gross less than a million dollars per year[2]! Do you want to be part of the 96% or do you want to be in that top 4%? Believe it or not, only 0.4% do more than $10 million[3][4] and it's up to you where you want to be.

What does it mean to be the best?

In this book, we will analyze what it really means and what the benefits are to be number one. That doesn't mean you have to compete with LA Fitness! You can succeed at any size when you set the right goals. This book will teach you how to create a seven-figure business, whether you are just starting or have been struggling for a while.

---

2 About the industry. (2010). Retrieved January 27, 2017, from http://www.ihrsa.org/about-the-industry/

3 Patrick, & hl, ? (2016, December 27). How to build a Billion dollar company - Patrick Bet-David Retrieved from http://www.patrickbetdavid.com/build-a-billion-dollar-company/

4 VALUETAINMENT (2016, December 27). How to build a Billion dollar company. Retrieved from https://www.youtube.com/watch?v=G1NowKSKuJ8

This book will answer the following questions:

- How do I separate myself from the crowd when the fitness industry is so saturated with gyms and personal trainers?
- How can I be the best in the business?
- How can I work on instead of in my business?
- How do I select a niche market?
- How do I market to this niche?
- How do I sell to my niche market?
- How do I train and hire a team with an effective hiring formula?
- How do I manage them and keep them on track?

A little bit about me

Who am I to tell you all of this?

I am Daniel Nyiri, CEO of 4U Fitness. I am a fitness professional and I have developed a high-tech invention that allows you to get a three-hour workout in just 20 minutes. We have been voted as the best gym and the most innovative business by many magazines and associations, and you may have also seen us on the hit TV show "The Doctors," where we showcased our equipment.

Currently we have been working towards preventing muscle atrophy so NASA can get our astronauts to safely colonize Mars!

I came to the United States in 2011 with just $150 in my pocket, not knowing anyone and not speaking English, besides "Hi, my name is Daniel and I am from Hungary." At the beginning, I had one goal: to open my own studio in less than two years. Once I had that goal, I had to write a plan for it otherwise it would stay just a dream. So I did. I worked five jobs simultaneously, day and night. Now we have a chain of studios with our own line of equipment and supplements, all of which we manufacture. We created an amazing academic system, the 4U Fitness University, to develop the best trainers in the industry.

The bottom line is, if I did it, you can do it too and I want to show you how to succeed in your business without any burnouts. At one point, I was working from 4:45 a.m. until 10 p.m. without a break. I ate while training. I had no friends and no life. If I knew then what I know now, I would have done things a lot differently – and been just as successful in much less time. Why am I sharing my secrets? I lost my grandparents to obesity and want to put an end to this epidemic. The more successful gyms there are, the more healthy people there will be. We are all in this together.

It's all about people, plan, execution and cash.

The goal of this book is to make you realize that you can no longer be a personal trainer. You are a business owner who needs to make it in a very competitive market. And that is simply not possible with you doing the training, unless you are planning on hiring someone to run the business while you are on the floor training clients. Even if you charge $100 per session and see 15 clients a day with 30-minute sessions, that is $1,500 per day x 6 days or 9,000 x 4 weeks to the tune of $36,000 per month or $432,000 per year. But you must have amazing skills in attracting, keeping, scheduling and so on with your clients to able to pull this off. You are still half a million short to enter the big leagues of seven figures. If we add in supplements, you get closer. But then what happens if you get in a car accident or get sick? I was absent for a month because of a surgery and my sales went up as planned because I had built contingency plans and built a fantastic team to work with.

You have to have the right system in place and you have to stop training clients. Yes, you heard me right. You have to quit training. Otherwise you won't be able to scale up your business. You are the captain of this ship. You are now all about team work. Working together as a team, you will pull it off, maintain your success and have some personal time as well.

CHAPTER 1

KEY MISTAKES THAT GYM OWNERS MAKE

"Experience is a hard teacher because she gives the test first, the lesson afterwards."

vernon Sanders Law

Many personal trainers are great at training clients, but not as great about running a business. When they suddenly become a business owner, they often focus on the wrong things and they look at the business backwards. Trainers need to let go of that personal training vantage point and switch to a strategic view.

These key mistakes can include:

- Just jumping in without any forethought or planning.
- Doing the exact same thing as before – personal training – while trying to pay the bills and clean the bathrooms. Working in the business instead of on the business.
- Not looking towards the future and not making plans for business growth.
- Giving up your personal life and other passions so that you can

work 24 hours a day.

- Buying gym or personal training studio when all you really want to do is train clients – instead, rent a space from an existing gym and work your butt off doing what you love. Get rid of your gym as soon as you can before you are forced to go out of business, because you cannot ignore all the needs of a new business

Have you made any of these mistakes? You need to stop working on the wrong things. If you simply want to focus on personal training, then you should work for someone else – not yourself. If you want to own a successful gym, you need to be an entrepreneur.

At this point, most trainers ask, "Does this mean I can't train clients anymore?" No, of course, you can! For pure joy, if nothing else. But it should not be the core of your business. It is only a problem when your training is consuming all the time needed to grow your business!

I have been there. I have worked all day, given up my personal life and gotten burned out. I have also heard many, many gym owners and personal trainers say that owning gym or personal training business will take away all your time and ruin your personal life. But it doesn't have to be that way. In the beginning, you definitely have to put in the work – the right work. You must run the business instead of letting the business run you.

Finally, it is important to recognize that you are not going to be able to charge more, be more successful, or attract more clients and become famous by collecting certifications. I have met many trainers who had so many but they didn't know how to scale upwards. They think certifications are the answer but they are not. This doesn't mean you should not be knowledgeable, you should absolutely be reading about your industry and up to date on all of the latest trends and news. You need to be out there so you can know what's going on and stay ahead of the game! If you think you don't have time to read or research because you're so busy working, then you need to reassess your goals. Do you want to be average or do you want to be the best?

CHAPTER 2: ———————

GET THE SCALE OUT

" You cannot solve a problem with the same level of thinking that created it."

Albert Einstein

Okay, I don't mean that kind of scale (although you should be taking care of your health – including regular exercise and a healthy diet – if you're going to own a successful gym)! I'm talking about scaling up.

In order to scale up, you need measure what you're doing and how you're doing it.

Business is just like training clients. You need to measure their progress to show results or you are doing it all wrong and you are just hoping for the best. The same goes for a business. If you don't measure your progress, you are just winging your business. One of our locations in Tampa Bay, FL is celebrating its 6th anniversary this year. From our studio door, we can see five different personal training studios. In a 10-mile radius, there are 68 gyms and personal training studios. And they all come and go. More than half of these have had different owners and managers; they close and reopen, close and reopen. Most of them aren't going to succeed because the owners are being run by their business. As an experiment, I called several local studios in the prime hours when a new client would call and I was only able to reach one out of 10 studios. How do you think a client would feel if they called and only got an answering machine over and over again? It's not a great first impression.

Scaling up requires measuring, learning and innovating. It comes down to tracking what is going well, finding where there is room for growth and always thinking of and planning for what is coming next.

Your results come down to your business activities. If you don't keep track and review your results month to month, there is no way you are going to make it. If you don't know how much money you have in your bank account or how many clients you have and what you need to succeed, your business will not work.

Always measure changes month to month and have at least 12 months of detailed accounting in front of you and compare and calculate changes in percentages that will measure growth to see what direction you are going -- up or down. Then find out why. If you are going down, find the solution and pin it down! It could be as simple as your trainers not taking payments on time. If you are going up, know why and make sure you continue fueling it!

Looking at the bottom number on a statement doesn't tell you anything – you have to analyze.

Here is an example:

Divide your personal trainers' total income and divide by the number of clients to get the per client cost. And see if you need to fix something. For example, if you pay your trainer after each client and you give out free trial sessions, this will show you what the real costs are of doing business per client. If you trainer does 10 free sessions and only one signs up while you pay them $16 per client, you end up paying a lot more than you think.

I also recommend calculating how effective you are in hiring new trainers and converting them into revenue makers. Just use revenue divided by trainer to determine your effectiveness percentage.

$$\frac{\text{Revenue}}{\text{Trainer}} = \text{\% Effectiveness}$$

What separates you from the competition?

Do you know what the only difference is between you and your competitions? No, it is not service or equipment. It's your management. Business don't fail because it's a bad business. Most of the time they fail because of the bad business owner and management.

It is time to change. Measure your results and look at the numbers. These numbers won't lie. Bad numbers equals bad management, while good numbers equal good management. Analyze your business every month and see what is draining you and how can you improve. You need to measure everything from phone calls to the number of paper towels used. The more detailed your information, the better.

When it comes to phone calls, for example, what time are they coming in? How many are you receiving? Who is calling? What are the calls about? How many of them are turning into real leads and consultations? How many turn into clients and how long do they stay? What is your total cost per client? This includes lead generation, phone service, employees, equipment used and so on. DATA IS KEY!

If you do what you have always done without measuring, changing and adapting, you will fail. You have to measure in order to see what to change and where to adapt.

At the beginning when you first build your gym, you will be the doer of everything --and this is necessary. You will do training, handle customer service, sales, consultations, build a website, create email campaigns, advertising and more. But then you need to learn how to delegate all these jobs to someone else so you can focus on scaling your business. If you add everything up, such as web design, sales, reception, training, cleaning and more, you will soon realize that you are doing work that is no longer worth your time. On top of that, it is really wearing you out and you cannot grow. Not to mention that your website probably won't look very professional!

You have to learn to let go, trust others and delegate. Your business will get stronger and you will be able to focus on the activities that matter most.

If you are just getting started, you might be excited about doing everything and working all of the time – taking on new clients, toiling from sunrise to sunset. But you need to delegate, scale up and trust in others if your business is to succeed. No one wants to work with a burned out personal trainer or business owner. Don't let your business, your dream take you over or run you down. It will be hard work but scaling and delegating will make everything that much easier.

If you're still wondering, "How is my business going to survive without me doing the work? Why would my clients come to train?" It's about the results. As a business owner, you can double accomplishments, while supporting your clients and your community. There is nothing better than creating many good-paying jobs while you help people reach their health and fitness goals.

CHAPTER 3: ——————————————————————

WELCOME YOUR COMPETITION WITH OPEN ARMS

"A hero is someone who has given his or her life to something bigger than oneself."

Joseph Campbell

You know you are making it and heading in the right direction when: your competitors start knocking on your door to train at your studio, when people from your industry, the industry experts come to learn from you. Welcome them in. You may be worried that they will steal your clients or your secrets. Here is the thing: They can try... but they don't have you.

We have many personal trainers and gym owners who train at our studios. I get even more phone calls and emails from out-of-state studio owners about our gyms and equipment. And sometimes I sell the equipment to them. They fly in, I teach them the basic training process and they take pictures and videos, which is totally fine with me because I know that they can't copy me or our business. They don't see how complex our business is or what is behind each appointment, free trial, consultation, and trainer. Each one of those has a million steps.

We have a great system that we teach, learn and follow. These other studio owners also assume that we have so many 5-star ratings on Yelp, Google and Facebook and hundreds of amazing transformational pictures and stories because we have a unique machine. They don't see all the work behind it. You may buy our machine, which is the most advanced training machine out there, but if you don't know what to do with it, what's the use? You need to learn the system. Most of the clients who train with us don't even know we have developed a unique workout system. They are just here for the results.

Our company gives out a free week trial, which includes a 45-minute consultation, a 45-minute full body assessment and strength and conditioning session, and a 45-minute session of your choice. But if you don't know why we do this and the science behind it, you won't be able to emulate our business' success.

What sets us apart?

- Our trainers go through a very rigorous hiring process and once they join the team, they go through our 4U Fitness University program, which takes three months. If they complete that successfully, scoring at least 90% on every assessment, then they can finally start training clients.
- We spent a year figuring out who is our avatar for the perfect personal trainer and how we get them. By working with Ph.D. students in Psychology, we came up with the right test to see if the trainers were right for our business. We never look for trainers anymore because now, the trainers come to us. We receive about 20 resumes per month. Last time I posted "We are hiring" on our Facebook page, we received more than 150 resumes in a week.
- We measure each trainer's work on a regular basis. Again, it comes back to knowing and understanding the numbers.

Business is a very complex sport! Even if a competitor takes some of your key people, they won't succeed as you will. A perfect example is the Russian Olympic hockey team. They have the most expensive and most talented players in the world, and everyone thinks they will win a gold medal when the winter Olympics roll around. But they don't have the system. Your competitors can take your information, but it doesn't mean they can take anything away from your business.

CHAPTER 4: ───────────

WHAT IS YOUR GOAL?

"People think focus means saying yes to the thing you've got to focus on. But that's not what it means at all. It means saying no to the hundred other good ideas that there are. You have to pick carefully. I'm actually as proud of the things we haven't done as the things I have done. Innovation is saying no to 1,000 things."

Steve Jobs

It all starts with a goal. What is your goal?

I assume you would like to own your own studio or, if you already own your own gym, you would like to have a seven-figure income. If you don't have a specific goal, then you're likely just getting by and will burn out very soon.

When it comes to having a clear goal, you have to understand how goals work and how you will know when you have achieved yours. Set a goal. Yes, your big goal can be to own a studio or gym that earns you a seven-figure income every year. But just writing that down on a piece of paper won't help. If your goal is to own and operate a seven-figure gym, you have to break it down all the way to see and understand what it will take to get there.

That is where a happiness alignment chart comes in[1]. You have to match your effort and your action with your goal or whatever it is you desire. Otherwise, if you just work and work without a goal, you are going nowhere.

Once you set your goal, it is time to come up with a plan. Without a plan, your goal is just a dream!

Set timelines and deadlines. Make sure you set realistic goals that you can actually achieve. Of course, you should reach high. That's exactly what I did and it worked beautifully – but my plan was always there to back up my goals and my actions. If you just write "In three years I will have a seven-figure income," it's just words. You need to back it up. You have to fill in the gaps.

I see several different types of trainers and gym owners today. There are the ones who are just starting out with a strong fire for success, so I call them the Hustlers. Then there are the gym owners who are barely getting by and they just not sure why they fail to attract and keep clients or why they are not making money – they are the Doers. As can be expected, there are plenty of gym owners who are burning out and, lastly, there are those who are making it, the Finishers; they have the clients and the money but they have no free time on their hands. Even though they are making it, their entire lives are dedicated to work, work, and more work.

The gym owners who are really, truly making it have finally realized it that it is time to measure and recreate what they do best and teach it to other people. Make sure this is a part of your goal and your plan – sharing the wealth and sharing your knowledge so that you can be even more successful.

This is yet another reason that you should fire yourself as a personal trainer. You have to have a laser focus on your goal and on your

---

1 Bet-David, P. (2016, October 11). How to be happy as an entrepreneur Retrieved from http://www.patrickbetdavid.com/how-to-be-happy-as-an-entrepreneur/

business. People who try to do everything will never make it. They will get lost and burned out in the process or, if they pull it off, it will just be a temporary success. Take Steve Jobs' word for it and accomplish on one thing at a time. Is it personal training? Is it growing your business? What is it? What is your goal? Set it, plan it, and then achieve it with laser focus in less time with amazing results.

CHAPTER 5:

WHY DO CLIENTS LEAVE?

"Losers have goals. Winners have systems."

Scott Adams

Why do clients leave?"

"Why do clients leave?" This is a too-common question in our industry. We often use excuses such as "training is too expensive" or "they just weren't serious," but there is always more to it. Hopefully, it will soon be something you no longer have to worry about.

What is your client retention rate? If someone truly likes something and sees the value in it, they will pay for it no matter what. We have had clients sell jewelry and other valuables to pay for training because they were so committed to their health. If a client stops coming, we have failed them and we need to know why.

Client retention is more important than new clients or training clients.

As a business owner, you should be far more concerned about your client retention rate than training clients. How do you think you will find more clients when you don't know why the current ones are leaving? Don't be afraid to ask and survey clients who are leaving; they will likely be very honest about their reasons for making a change and you can use this information to improve your practices.

Your clients might be leaving because you never answer the phone. They might be leaving because they feel you're more focused on finding new clients than working with the current ones. They might be leaving because they aren't getting the results they want. You need to know why before you can turn the ship around, so make it a point to understand why clients are leaving – and then focus on the ones who are staying.

Often, the problem is that business owners and managers think the only way to be successful is to grow through new customers. More and more. Instead of monitoring the ones you already have. Focus on the customers you have now, giving them the greatest experience possible, and you will grow without even having to advertise – it's called word of mouth and it's the best way to get new clients – referrals from people who already love your business.

In summary, make sure you are tracking your client retention and attribution rates. Maintaining the clients you have – and turning them into lifelong fans – is the best way to grow your business.

WORK HARD, BUT DON'T WORK ALL THE TIME

"Being busy is a form of laziness - lazy thinking and indiscriminate action. Being busy is most often used as a guide for avoiding the few critically important but uncomfortable actions."

Tim Ferris

Maybe you don't have the issue of client attribution but you do have the challenge of complete exhaustion. Your clients control your schedule and you are working ALL OF THE TIME. I have been there, so I completely understand where you are coming from.

I always wanted to be a leader and I have always been passionate about health and wellness. But I didn't truly earn the title of CEO until my business took off and I earned the respect of my team and their clients. I felt official when "Entrepreneur" magazine called me a CEO and when "Business Observer" compared me to Elon Musk and Steve Jobs, but that didn't happen overnight. And even then, I knew we are heading in the right direction but I also knew that I had to work even harder and smarter.

Being completely booked is nothing to brag about. If you are training and working all day, then who is answering the phones? How do you take new clients? Who runs consultations? Who is following up with old leads or clients who left? Who keeps your clients on track? And most importantly, how do you grow? Or what happens if you get sick? Can you even think about vacation?

If any of these questions make you worry, then you have some work to do. Here is the good news: you already have an amazing service! However, there is always some bad news: there are thousands of companies who also had the most amazing product ever and they went out of business because they were so busy on their product that they didn't think about growing. You cannot sustain this.

When people reach out to me, they often start by saying, "You must be incredibly busy." And I always respond that I'm really not. Not because I am not in charge of my time and life. When people say "busy," that implies out of control to me. Think about it, we all have the same amount of time in a given day or week. However, some people manage hundreds, even thousands of employees, and billions of dollars and they still have time to go out, have dinner, relax, read and enjoy their lives. Too many of the gym owners I meet today don't even have time for a cup of coffee – let alone time to read a book, take a vacation or enjoy a night out. Again, this is because their business is controlling them and their time, rather than the other way around!

Great operators get burned out, while great business owners get rich.

Let's say that you are doing pretty well. You have everything in order. You have hired a great team of personal trainers and you have stopped training completely but are still doing the operations. That's great, you are one step closer to firing yourself and becoming a successful business owner who can step back from operations and hire someone to manage this aspect of your business in your place.

I think we can all agree hiring your first trainer or employee of any kind is the scariest but maybe the most fun part of your business. It's a clear signing of growing and advancing forward.

Even better, you are getting to know yourself better and you have recognized that you are more than a personal trainer now, you are a manager.

At this point, you are starting to get your life back. The business is running itself. Your trainers are working by themselves. You feel good about everything. This is when it always happens! You are checking your emails or social media or receive a phone call and there it is – one of your clients is very unhappy and is complaining loudly. Naturally, a group of clients will show up at the same time. Or you will have a double booking or a trainer will arrive late. Then you see your trainer doing something wrong with clients, maybe it's not paying attention to their form or talking too much, so you give them a gentle correction. All of a sudden, clients are leaving and starting to ask for their money back. Consultations are not signing up anymore. You ask "what happened?"

You will probably be tempted to over-coach your trainers at this point – tell them how you would do things, start watching them like a hawk, and maybe even join in on the personal training sessions again. And just like that, you're stepping back into your old role. This almost always happens. But you don't have to fall victim to this scenario. It is not your trainers, it is not the economy, not the high-maintenance clients, not the machines. It is you.

This is when you need to shine as a manager and leader. If you keep doing the same things, you will end up at the same place and you will go nowhere. You need to develop leadership skills, which are even more important in times of crisis.

It's all about working smarter, staying cool under pressure and creating the right business culture – for your staff, for your clients, for your own personal growth.

Hire away

As a business owner, you need to focus on one job and one job only: business owner. That means that you can't be a manager and you can't be a personal trainer. You need to hire those positions out and fill them with the best candidates available.

Make sure you assign the right job roles and responsibilities to the right people, focus on your employees' strengths and assets and make assignments accordingly.

At our studios, we have one person responsible for all leads and scheduling, another person responsible for consultations, and another for free week trials and turning those into sales. And we have a manager who keeps them accountable. If any of the above people turn in their monthly report sheets and something doesn't look right, the manager has to be able to fix that. He/she creates accountability, which includes addressing issues but still celebrating successes and achievements. A logical chain of command, clear roles and responsibilities, and a tracking system are all essential to your business' success – and to ensuring that you don't work every hour of every day.

Make sure you provide value every step of the way – in every service and interaction.

Once you have done that and have finished your operation manual, you will be able to hire people with an average skill set. You can hire people with a basic PT certification and teach them your system and all they have to do is follow your ordinary yet amazing working system. Instead of hiring for skills and certifications, hire for your core values and culture!

Once you have this all figured out you need to make sure that your trainers deliver exceptional and consistent service. Your studios should have a familiar feel. This is about creating a culture. It entails matching uniforms (that your staff actually like and want to wear!), listening to feedback from both staff and clients, and showing you care in everything you do.

If you have all this in order, your clients should be very happy because you have a working, consistent system where every single time they come in they will receive the same amazing experience.

Set the right tone

How can you establish a mission and vision if you are too busy training or managing? You can't. As a leader, you are responsible for hiring the right people, imparting your vision and then letting your employees shine. You will still need to coach your managers and key people. Initially you should be able to offer one-on-one coaching and development sessions where you focus on strengths, opportunities and next steps.

During coaching sessions, you will help your team come up with goals of their own. By the way, you should never tell them what you want. You should make them want to do it by themselves. There is a difference. If you tell someone, I want you to get 10 clients by the end of the month, that's telling – it's not very inspirational. Instead, give them a choice and encourage them to do the impossible. Ask, "Do you think you can get 10 clients by the end of the month?" If they agree, then it's their choice – not yours. Your employees will be far more successful when they are truly invested in their goals.

Along those lines, make sure that you place a priority on these coaching sessions – try to never cancel (if you ever do so, it must be for a very good reason or your employees will think they aren't important). Schedule a full hour for each employee per month. If you think you need more than one per month, then schedule 30-minute sessions more frequently. At these meetings, you should focus on goal-setting, expectations and next steps. Come up with a precise plan so there is no confusion. At subsequent meetings, you can discuss process more than results to keep the conversation flowing. Always give detailed feedback on their performance and do not hold back anything. Confronting issues head-on and in a timely manner will prevent bad habits from forming.

All of this work and dedication will ensure that you can enjoy work while you are there, but that you still have time to enjoy family and friends, hobbies and life away from the gym as well.

CHAPTER 7: ——————————

WORK OUT
YOUR BRAIN

"If you let your learning lead to knowledge, you become a fool. If you let your learning lead to action, you become wealthy!."

Darren Hardy

When the reporter for the "Chicago Tribune" called to discuss making my first million, I referred back to one of my role models, investor and businessman Warren Buffett. I said: "Buffett says that he reads at least four hours per day. If you want to be a millionaire, you have to be the best at something, and the only way to get ahead is to keep feeding your mind."

It's reported that Buffett spends much of his day reading newspapers, books, financial statements and reports. Granted, the average person can't devote most of the day to reading. What you can do, however, is take advantage of every learning opportunity, such as:

* Attending business and investment conferences and seminars
* Taking online courses
* Finding a business mentor
* Reading 15-30 minutes per day

As an entrepreneur and business owner, you have one job. Advance forward, know what you want. This means that you should have a plan for 10 years from now; when you know exactly what you want, you can begin to build it backwards. Adjust everything to make that plan the reality. Construct it.

Your job is to prepare your business and yourself for growth. Ask yourself the right questions. What do I want this company to become? When? What will it take to get there? How much equipment and how many people do I need? How big does my gym need to be to support all of this? Do I need more than one location? When you craft the answer to these important questions, then you can plan it out. All businesses without a plan will fail, end of story. Without a plan, you are just winging it and have no idea what is going to happen next. Keep your mind sharp and your plan moving forward.

Let your business serve the rest of your life

Why do 9 out of 10 gym owners fail to find a mentor, attend seminars, read, research and create a plan?

The problem is that most of this gym owners started out as personal trainers, so they focus on things to be done instead of what the business should be doing. An owner will ask how is the business working and the personal trainer will ask what work needs to be done. The personal trainer looks only on the inside for income from personal training clients. The entrepreneur looks at the entire business from the outside for overall results.

At some point, you should realize that your purpose in life is not to serve your business, it is actually the opposite. Your business' purpose is to serve your life and then finally you can go to work on your business instead in your business. You will have more free time, more money, and a better life.

That's what this chapter is all about – making yourself a better person and making your business and community better in turn. When you learn new skills, read about new ideas and connect with others, you build that capacity. You have the vision and the ability to communicate it. You stay focused on personal and business growth – you regularly check on your plans and goals and reflect that back to the culture and vision of the company. You need to able to replicate your business as an entrepreneur. This means everything should be systemized and able to run without you. You could open 10, 100 or 10,000 locations the same way because you have a working system for the business itself and for the employees in it. A good gym owner never stops learning. A good gym owner reads books and analyzes the market daily. A good gym owner never stops adapting to new technology and innovations. Simply put, when you get better, your business gets better, too.

WHAT IS YOUR NICHE?

"Don't be afraid of being different be afraid of being the same as everyone else."

unknown

By now, you've probably asked and answered a lot of questions. This is part of assessing whether you want to be a personal trainer or a gym owner.

And here is the most important question to ask and answer:

Why are you doing this? What is the purpose? Are you doing this for the money? Are you solving any problems? Are you doing this for passion? Is there a real specific reason? Did someone die in your family from obesity and you made your life mission to put a stop on obesity? What is the real reason? You have to have a real reason that will keep you motivated and keep you up at night because you are so passionate about it that you cannot stop thinking about it. You cannot start a gym or any type of business without a reason behind it. And it better be more than just money. People who start businesses strictly for money purposes have the highest rate of failure.

I want you to really think about your WHY before you move forward with this book. The next chapter is about your pitch. And without having a strong WHY, your pitch won't come to life! You really need to think about this. What moves you? If you don't have a strong WHY, you are not going to make it. If you can't figure out your WHY, starting a gym or continuing to run your gym is not for you! It is not too late to start over. Life is short to spend it on things that you don't love.

I want you to write down your WHY right now; then check back every other month to keep yourself on track and remind yourself of that powerful why:

Once you know your WHY, then it is time to figure out who your target clientele is, where to find them and how to attract them. Here are some tips to help with that:

- Find a problem and solve it. To be successful in this crowded market, you need to look for a problem and create its solution! For example, we came up with a solution for the common "I have no time to exercise" excuse. We developed a high-tech machine that gives powerful results in just 20 minutes. We target professional women who have kids- because these women are incredibly busy and juggle a lot of demands, our machine is just what they need. We help them achieve their goals with two, 20-minute sessions per week and guarantee their results or their money back. It's a perfect niche for us.
- Continue to generate leads and then work them. We generate more than 80 good leads per month, per studio. These leads become clients and combined with referrals, help us grow organically.

I wish I recognized my niche market when I first started. At the beginning, I was a trainer to athletes, celebrities, mothers, fathers, kids, you name it. I got a maximum of 10 leads per month and I was working too hard. One night I sat down and started to work on my target market. I analyzed my current clientele and realized my target client is the entrepreneurial mom, so I developed a program for her and went for it. We offer a rewarding referral program to bring in the husbands and friends thus creating, the perfect system.

Determine your ideal clientele and be very, very specific!

I looked at the numbers. Ninety percent of moms are online versus only 76% of women, and 64% of mothers[1] ask their mom friends before they would commit to a personal trainer. Three-quarters of all moms want to be part of a special selected program or team and 92% will pass on the information to at least one friend. In addition, 55% of active daily social media moms make their purchases[2] based on a friend review or social media recommendation. By 2028, the average American women is expected to earn more than the average American man. Not to mention that women control 51% of all private wealth[3] in the United States and they also control 60% of all personal wealth. An average woman spends more than $500 per month[4] on health and fitness whereas an average male only spends about $200. Each of these numbers were very striking and meaningful to me.

All of this means that our niche market is mothers who have two or more kids and spend money on their kids, and have very little time to spare. Based on my analysis, out of the $10 billion market of personal

1 Silverstein, M. J., & Sayre, K. (2009, September 1). The female economy. Retrieved January 27, 2017, from Gender, https://hbr.org/2009/09/the-female-economy

2 Lewis, M. (2013, November 20). Student credit cards. Retrieved January 27, 2017, from http://www.moneycrashers.com/men-vs-women-shopping-habits-buying-decisions

3 Female factor - women by the numbers. (2016). Retrieved January 27, 2017, from http://www.thefemalefactor.com/statistics/statistics_about_women.html

4 G, A. How much money do Americans spend on fitness products each year? Retrieved January 27, 2017, from https://www.quora.com/How-much-money-do-Americans-spend-on-fitness-products-each-year

training, moms with two kids or more represent 8% of the total personal training contributors, however, they account about 3 % of all personal training purchases[5].

Once you identify and recognize your market, then you can determine where to find them.

Great companies are not great because they are for everyone. They are after a very small market. And they are all about delivering the absolute best service tailored for their very small, but fanatical group of fans and devotees. If you think about it, we only focus on 8% of the total fitness market and we completely ignore the remaining 92%.

Apple is also after one niche market. They are only after the people who are okay with closed architecture! There are so many Android and Windows users out there who find that annoying, yet they remain one of the most valuable and respected companies in the world.

What is your niche market? You have to identify this before you can go further. That is just the first step. Then you have to tailor EVERYTHING around this niche and know exactly how to market to them. Before we figured this out, we spend thousands of dollars on marketing and received very few leads in return. Once we analyzed the data focused on exactly what we wanted for our business, we nailed it! Now we get between 50-90 leads per month. At some of our locations we have a waiting list to get in!

I recommend that you take the time look at your current clientele at your studios and figure out who is your main clientele, then figure out how your company is already attracting these people. Are these the people you and your company want to attract and keep? If yes, why, how did you, and how should you attract them? Why did they pick your place among all of the others out there?

Start asking these questions and write down all the answers. It doesn't

---

5 Miller, M. (2014, January 18). How much money 4 women spend on health and wellness each month. Retrieved January 27, 2017, from http://www.womenshealthmag.com/health/wellness-

hurt to ask all your trainers about their clientele as well. Collect as much data as you can and then analyze your marketing strategy. Once you know who you are attracting and who you want to attract, you can go after it and build the right plan for your business and your niche – this includes your website, landing page, ad campaigns, referral programs and even workouts specifically designed for this niche market. For example, new mothers want to lose weight and body fat quickly so that they can get back to their previous weight and size pre-pregnancy. Therefore, it would only make sense to design your programs to these needs, with a focus on losing belly fat, tightening up that booty and focusing on body confidence. Now you can sit with your team and come up with the perfect program designed for these mothers. In addition, your staff will do the same, so if anyone leaves or gets sick, you have another staff member who knows exactly how you work and what needs to be done. Everyone is doing the same thing and on the same page. Why do you think Southwest Airlines only has ONE TYPE of airplane in its fleet? That's right, they have only one type of plane! It is so they can save on the parts when they need to replace something and they can have any crew member jump in when needed since all of the airplanes are exactly the same. They do not need to hire and train staff differently for different type of airplanes since they only have one type, which means that they can afford to employ far less employees to fly and maintain the company's aircraft. Smart, right!? Companies like Southwest Airlines are great role models, regardless of the industry you are in.

You have to be unique and you need to learn from the big sharks who have been around for a long time and own a significant percentage of the marketplace in your industry. You have to recognize and connect with your niche. Attending expos is great, but if you are at a fishing conference and your target market is actually airplanes, then you are wasting your time.

Set up shop where your niche market is. Let them know how important they are to you and treat them right.

Don't try to be everything to everyone

The bottom line is that you simply can't take on everyone who comes through your front door! You can't call yourself "the everything" gym. Even Amazon, "the everything store," started with a small niche market until they became the giant of that small market of online book sales! And eventually they became the everything store, which took lots of time, money, and thousands of hard-working, dedicated employees. "Everyone" is not your market. You probably know that already. So who is your market? Why do you want to serve them? What opportunity awaits you? Make sure you can answer all of these questions before you proceed.

WIND UP FOR A SERIOUS PITCH

"Success is the sum of small efforts, repeated day-in and day-out."

Robert Collier

Once you have determined your ideal niche market, then it is time to make your pitch to them. You need to know what drives this particular group of people and how to talk to them in person, on your company website, through social media, videos, blog posts and more. At this point, you must develop a pitch that you and every single person at your gym can memorize, share and repeat word for word. This includes your receptionist, accountant and especially your trainers – every single employee should know and align with your pitch!

When I first meet with a new gym owner and their team, I encourage each employee to introduce himself or herself and ask them what they do every day. Every single gym I have visited so far has failed at this simple task (including my own at the beginning, until I stumbled upon the incredibly important concept of the pitch).

Typically, when I ask each employee at a particular personal training facility or gym about who they are and what they do, they all said something different. They generally like to stand out, which means they will share crazy titles and certifications and all these things up front to let me know that they are the experts. This is not a good strategy to begin with. You need to start low and slowly build it up your expertise and credentials – never oversell yourself.

You need to be very clear about who you are and what you do. You have less than 20 seconds to grab a person's attention and if you start listing off every single certification and title, you will go nowhere (not to mention that the person you are talking to will quickly tune you out if you are all about lists and certifications. You have to connect on a more emotional level to keep someone's attention.).

When I meet anyone for the first time, I usually ask them what they do. Honestly, I will even do this in an elevator, just to learn more about the people I'm standing next to. It's good to learn and to remember that you are always pitching! Everywhere! And you get what you pitch for. How many times have people asked you what you do? And out of those times, how many times did you acquire a new client, buyer or whatever market you are pitching? As I said before, you will get what you pitch for.

When I meet someone, I always ask them what they do. They will say their thing, and I will respond with, "That's awesome" Typically, they will then ask what I do and I say:" I am Daniel Nyiri, CEO of 4U Fitness. I am a personal trainer and we developed a high-tech invention that allows you to get a three-hour workout in just 20 minutes." After this, they generally say, "What? A three-hour workout in just 20 minutes! Sign me up! Is that for real? How does it work?" I love the responses I receive from my pitch and I love delivering it. Do you see the point? I clearly and slowly stated my name and title so they know who they are talking and I downplayed my role by saying that I am a personal trainer instead of saying I am a fitness expert. Now that is a recipe for disaster because then they would probably ask, "What makes you the expert?" You should never say that you are an expert -- let other people call you that and let the person you talk to decide if you are one or not! Play it simple and cool (and, of course, being a personal trainer is pretty cool). Then, I can really grab their attention when I say, "We developed a high-tech invention that allows you to get a three-hour workout in just 20 minutes." SOLD!

Now is the time when you move on to creditability! At this point, you can state your gym's accomplishments. For example, here is something I enjoy sharing with people:

"Yes, it is for real. As a matter fact, we were voted as the best gym in the entire Bay area and you may have also seen us on the TV show 'The Doctors' where we showcased our equipment. Currently, we have been busy working towards preventing muscle atrophy so NASA can get our astronauts to safely colonize Mars!" It's not a bad elevator speech!

And did you see what I did again? I started out with the smallest detail and built it up again towards the biggest accomplishment, this is something a lot of people fail to do. They start with the biggest deal and backtrack from there, so that their big accomplishment gets minimized by the other details. Make sure you know how to peak people's interest when you share your pitch.

The next step is to identify the problems that you are fixing for them. You will likely modify this depending on who you are speaking to. For example, if you are pitching to a group of investors instead of potential future clients, you will update your pitch. You can let those investors know that you have analyzed the three main problems in the health and fitness industry and created a solution for them, building your company around this promise.

This speech goes something like this:

People today face three main problems in regards to staying healthy:

1. We live in a fast-paced world and finding time to work out is now harder than ever.

2. We also live in a convenient world, which makes eating healthy,

nutritious foods harder than ever when unhealthy options are simply an arm's reach away.

3. We live in an impatient world and most people don't see the results fast enough and quickly lose their motivation.

Your investors will clearly understand the problem and possibly see themselves somewhere along the way as well.

So the next question is, how do we fix these problems? What is the solution!?

Our solution to you us:

- We solve these problems through our scientifically based workouts that save you time by only taking 20 minutes of your time twice per week.

- We complement these workouts with easy-to-follow nutritional advice that accelerates the results from the workouts so that our clients stay more motivated than ever before.

And now is the time when you bring in the real reason WHY you are doing this. Most of the time people ask, but even if they don't, you need to share this information with depth and emotion so they understand how dedicated you are to helping other people. Never say something like "I am doing this because I love doing this." That's great, but you need a real reason that will touch someone's heart. This is why it is so important that every single employee develops their own WHY and believe in it.

My personal WHY is the following:

The reason why I am so committed to helping people stay fit is because every 90 seconds, one person dies from obesity. I lost my grandfather to diabetes and grandmother to obesity. I never want to see another person experience this kind of loss and sadness over something that is entirely preventable.

You need to find a reason like that. Most people who get into business usually have a strong reason and a touching why behind them and that what makes them so successful and gives them the fire when they need it the most! Find that fire and use it!

The last part is one, concise sentence that you state at the end that sums up all of the information you have shared and everything you want someone else to remember.

Ours is: We are known as the inventors of the No Excuses Workout Solution.

After you have done all this, you will have no problem attracting new customers, investors and fans. Your team will benefit greatly and your culture will grow as well.

It is critical that everyone at your company understands your vision and your pitch.

Here is how it all works together:

Clarity:
I am Daniel Nyiri CEO of 4U Fitness. I am a fitness professional and we developed a high-tech invention that allows you to complete a three-hour workout in 20 minutes. (For the working or busy individual who has limited time).

Credibility:
We were voted as the Best Gym in the entire Bay Area. You may have also seen us on the hit TV show "The Doctors" where we showcased our equipment.

Currently we have been very busy working towards preventing muscle atrophy so NASA can get our astronauts to safely colonize Mars.

Problem:
1. People today face three main problems in regards to staying healthy:
2. We live in a fast-paced world and finding time to work out is now

harder than ever.

3. We live in a convenient world which makes eating healthy, nutritious foods harder than ever when unhealthy options are simply an arm's reach away.

4. We live in an impatient world and most people don't see the results fast enough and they lose their motivation

Solution:

We solve these problems through our scientifically based workouts that save you time by only taking 20 minutes of your time twice per week. We complement these workouts with easy-to-follow nutritional advice that accelerates the results from the workouts so our clients stay more motivated than ever before.

Why:

The reason why I am so committed to helping people stay fit is because every 90 seconds one person dies from obesity. I lost my grandfather to diabetes and grandmother to obesity. I never want to see another person experience this kind of loss and sadness over something that is entirely preventable.

Mission:

We are known as the inventors of the No Excuses Workout Solution. Now create yours and practice it, every day! When you getting ready in the morning, driving your car and before going to sleep. Once you have this memorized and know it inside and out, then you can practice with others. Introduce yourself in the elevator, restaurants and at events, and ask others what they do. It will get the ball rolling and give you the chance to share your story and your why. Go to networking events and practice! Ask people what they think and modify if you need to.

Now that you know why are you doing this, who your niche market is and understand how to deliver a perfect pitch, it is time to get the word out!

CHAPTER 10:————————————

GET THE WORD OUT

"Start where you are. Use what you have. Do what you can."

Arthur Ashe

I studied a lot of successful people on my own road to success (and I highly recommend that you do the same). I stumbled upon Regis McKenna, the author of "Relationship Marketing: Successful Strategies for The Age of the Customer" who shares the marketing secrets of Steve Jobs and Andy Grove, a famous entrepreneur from hometown and country Budapest, Hungary. In his book, McKenna says that the first thing you should do is set one hour aside each week to work on your marketing strategies. Second, and most important in my opinion, is to set a list of the top 25 influencers in your market. During the week, you should then spend that hour figuring out how you are going to market to this list of the 25 top influencers. Since you have your pitch ready, you should have no problem convincing these influencers to help you. The more influential people you put on the list, the more chances you have to scale your business bigger and faster. On my list, for example, the most influential person was two-time Miss Olympia, Erin Stern. At that time when I made the list, no one really knew about me or my business. I was just a little personal trainer still working in my business most of the time instead of on my business. However, I reached my tipping point when I decided to scale it up, step back, and work only on my business and growing it into a big empire.

Inspired by this book and a few early successes, I started to reach out to these people, including Erin Stern. I used Instagram, email, Facebook, Twitter and even in-person outreach. As you can imagine, no one really want to deal with you when you are a nobody – not to mention a 24-year-old nobody still learning how to speak English. But I didn't give up and neither should you!

And I'm glad I didn't. I am not sure if Erin remembers when we first started to talk; it took about 18 months of my persistence in contacting her before she returned my correspondence. And now, she is our spokesmodel. Once she learned about our business and what we do, she was impressed and said that she did not want to miss out on this amazing journey. We are incredibly grateful, since she has opened up many doors for us because she is well known and liked in the fitness industry – not to mention that she is regularly on the cover of "Women's Health", "Shape" and many other magazines. So make your list and don't be shy about it! Don't listen to the doubters who laugh at your list. Don't let anyone influence your self-confidence or tell you that someone is out of your league. Don't let people talk you out of this. You can do it. Aim high! If you aim low, you will get low. If you aim high, you get high. It's that simple! Naturally, you need to work at this regularly, learn to not take no for an answer and shake it off when someone tells you that you are just "lucky" when you start to achieve some real success. Put in the time and it will pay off.

Honestly, I prefer this method of marketing to advertising in newspapers or magazines, which may or may not reach my target clients and will cost me a lot of money. That kind of advertising can be helpful if it's one tool in your kit, but you need to think bigger than just paid advertisements.

Google yourself

Now is a good time to Google your name if you haven't done so already. There is nothing wrong with this practice and you should be doing it regularly. Most of your clients will do it, too.

How do you measure? What comes up? Make sure you fix any problems or issues before they turn into something bigger. Take down those party pictures on Facebook – it's time to be professional now. If you Google Daniel Nyiri, you will find everything that you need to know about me, which simply lends greater credibility to my business. Once upon a time, you would have come across a lot of pictures of me in Calvin Klein underwear from my modeling era. This worked pretty well for me when I was a personal trainer. Today, however, you have to scroll thorough quite a few pages on Google to find those pictures and you will see more of me in business attire, which is the way I want it.

Go ahead google yourself. If nothing comes up, you need to fix that! Does your business come up? By the way, when I pick a doctor or personal trainer, attorney or any other person to hire, if I don't find anything on the internet about them, I move on.

Once you done any fixing or updating, you need to start working on your online profile. Be active on all social media sites and use lots of pictures and catchy text on your websites. Make sure to use keywords to your name and business on all of your pictures as well, which makes it easier for Google and other search engines to find them. How many features do you have? International or any local? You need to work on that. Once you get in magazines and TV shows, that will help boost your profile since their websites have millions of visitors daily.

Are you on YouTube? You need to be! Use Facebook Live to your advantage; you can reach all your followers with it and you can connect them on a personal level through a series of videos. Host an FAQ and see how many people will respond. I recommend having a friend ask a couple questions to get the ball rolling.

Even if you only have a handful of viewers, people still get notified you were that live and they can see it later. It's all about building your profile and reputation – also known as free advertising

Make sure to post every day, at least two times, on all social media sites. If people see that you only post once a month or so, they will quickly lose interest in you and your business. In addition, you need to give out free and entertaining information so people come back for more. Upload four valuable posts for every one promotion.

While you do have to sell, you should not be selling all of the time. We have thousands of readers every day who go to our websites for our recipes; our business now has more than 150 healthy home-cooked recipes with full cooking instructions and macros with pictures and videos on how to make them and we give them away for free. We also share a variety of informational posts on why people should eat differently and work out. This is useful information but it's still colorful and entertaining. Then we post some funny and goofy posts, especially outtakes from our trainers. On top of that, we also post many transformational stories with interesting, valuable content and pictures. It's all about creating value, driving interest and keeping people coming back for more because they know your business offers useful and fun information.

Make sure that every single thing you post on your social media sites is linked back to your website. Speaking of your website, how is that going? Do you have a professional website that generates leads for you? Or did you make it yourself? If that is the case, then you really need to hire someone to develop a new website. Have a professional do it. A professional can create a clean look and layout, metrics that test your ads, calls to action, a simple navigation and a website that makes money for you.

We always use three different landing pages on our website so we can test what pictures, videos, text or colors work. We analyze this data each month and use the one that works the most and then we keep on testing. Our website brings a lot of leads in to our studio. It took me five tries to find the perfect company to design and run our website – it wasn't easy but it was worth the process. Since then, it has been an amazing relationship and we work together well as a team. It is almost like they are part of 4U Fitness. If you Google "Mike Arce and Daniel Nyiri GSD Show," you will find out all the details in a 60-minute interview on what to do with your marketing and how to find the right team for you! This free video will save you both time and money.

Add it up

You can't just put stuff out there and hope for the best. You have to measure your marketing and advertising efforts.

This means that you have to systemize everything and you have to track everything, including details such what times are people calling, what times do they answer calls in return, who are you attracting, what ads/marketing promotions are working and what ones aren't and pretty much every other aspect of your business. For example, we found out that calling mothers to book appointments is perfect around 10 a.m. because that is when they are often free after dropping off kids; however, it is not such a great ideal to call after 5 p.m., since it is time for dinner, baths, homework and family time. But for single business women, on the other hand, we have better success when we call after 6 p.m. because they are often home and available at that time.

Granted, all of this requires work and practice, but it will make your business stronger. It is another avenue for marketing and making connections. When you are calling leads or clients, you and your staff must have a script both for talking with someone and for leaving a message.

Work on your website

A professional website can be as expensive as building a store, but it can be just as valuable! If you just want to get a beautiful website that gives you creditability and gives people an easy way to find you and see that you are the real deal, then your business is already a winner. Just have a basic simple and beautiful website. Focus on that and slowly build the rest around it as you and your business evolve.

If you have amazing landing pages like we do, your website is ready for SEO (search engine optimization); this makes it even easier for people to find you and make referrals. Customize your landing pages and test, test, and test more until you find the right one for your business.

Of course, you are only allowed to work on your website if you have figured out your niche market! Without that there is no point because you don't know who you are going after. Are you marketing to big, beefy guys or moms and busy, professional women? Your website – including the photos and the text – must reflect that or you will quickly turn your niche off if they see someone who doesn't reflect their goals on your home page.

Ultimately, the bottom line is that your website has to appeal to your clientele. If, for instance, you know that your facility has an expertise in working with high-performing athletes, then your website has to be built around that. If it is working moms, then it should to be all about them.

Remember this: less is more! Use pictures, videos and a small amount of text on the main page. You need to build a website in a way that makes it very simple for the client who is seeing it for the first time; they need enough information to take the next step but not so much that they get overwhelmed.

This means that you do not need to include a full list of services, your certifications, background or anything like that on the main page. People will lose interest if you overload them with too much information. All they really want to know is: what can you offer them, why should they join, and why now? If you answer these questions, you will draw them in. Try to use your pitch to build the website and start building it down like the way they scroll down on a page. Start with general information and at the very bottom you finish up with the specific details. Make sure that you include a clear call to action on the way so that someone can sign up for a one-week trial or a free appointment.

Network the right way

If you want to grow your brand and have people talk about you and know who you are, you need to get your name out there. One of the easiest ways to do so is having your pitch down really well and attending social events where you meet other business professionals. I highly recommend you try to find networking events where your client would hang out; you will likely attract new clients this way.

If you are at a business event, then your focus should be mainly on building your brand. Of course, you need to do this. There is nothing more valuable than when a highly successful businessperson who has become your client starts to introduce you to his/her peers. They are instantly sold! This is why the golden rule is that you never turn down an invitation from your client. They will be so happy to invite you out and introduce you to all of their friends. Any time we went to an event like that, we walked away with three to five new clients. And those clients stay forever and ever unless you mess something up.

Look on your local Chamber of Commerce's website for new business openings, and then go out there and introduce yourself to the new business owner. You can give him or her a deal and say that all of their new customers will receive a free session or whatever you deal or promotion you decide to offer. You just have to make sure it's free, without a catch and has a deadline (for instance, they need to come in in the next seven days or they lose it) and it should definitely have some real value. Ask some of your clients to go check out this new business, and, in return, you can give them a free session. Make sure you tell these clients to mention your business and that you sent them over. This is a great way to set up a new connection and it can pay off now and in the future.

You also did your good deed for the day – helping out a local business and your clients – so that is a win-win in anybody's book.

BONUS: ————————————

SHAPE UP YOUR ONLINE PRESENCE

By Mike Arce, CEO of Loud rumor

Online marketing has become more important than ever. Whenever you get your hands on this book, it's probably event more important than the day I decided to write this. The trend is that online marketing is constantly becoming the #1 way to advertise your business.

In particular, social media advertising has become even more important than Google, Bing, and Yahoo advertising - AKA search advertising - in certain fields such as the fitness industry. More specifically, this really applies to fitness studios that want to get more paying members through the door. Unfortunately, there aren't enough people looking online for a fitness studio to go to. But if we can find them and provide some really great compelling offers, we can actually lure them into our studio even though this wasn't top of mind.

In order to do that, you want to make sure it's done right and professionally. This means you need to think about the entire journey that someone goes through for your advertising process.

So first, is this person the right fit? Are they the ideal customer that you'd really like to target? To find this out, look at your current customers and determine who your top members are. Figure out what makes them who they are and create a template of that person. Then advertise specifically to people like that.

For example, are they between the ages of 30 and 50? Do they live within a certain mile radius of your studio? Do they like organic food? Are they moms?

You can actually target things like this on Facebook to make sure your ads get seen by the right person.

Then comes the offer. The offer is the most important part of your ad. Promoting 50% off of a year long membership isn't nearly as attractive as a free week. In fact, a free week has been proven to be the best offer that we've ran and tested with over 140 independent gyms and studios. Once someone sees your ad, make sure the imagery speaks to them. So if you want to promote your fitness studio to women between 40 and 50 years old, don't show them a picture of a 21 year old in phenomenal college shape. Make sure you really match people in the image with people you want to target so they feel like they're in the right place and not intimidated.

Now once they click on your Facebook ad, the videos and all other assets on your landing pages should match that as well. Make sure you have a fluid process. You can learn more about tips like this by watching The GSD Show where there's tons of different guests who talk about the different ways to market and advertise your fitness business (as well as other challenges).

I had the opportunity to sit on stage with Marcus Lemonis to talk about the fitness business. In particular, we covered funnels and the importance of getting funnels in place for your business. For those that don't know what a funnel is, it's basically when someone sees your ad and raises their hand to say "I want to learn more about this offer!" Then each step of the process after that ad takes them to a different step that gets them closer to becoming a buyer. That's the funnel.

I truly believe in funnels. ClickFunnels is an amazing tool you can use to create landing pages and funnels just like this. The owner of ClickFunnels, Russell Brunson, wrote an amazing book called DotCom Secrets that I encourage every person to read who wants to get into the internet marketing game.

Whatever you chose to do, just always keep one thing in mind.

It's important to learn and stay up to date with internet trends. It's becoming the biggest part of everyone's business, and those who aren't using it are falling short and going out of business. Those who do use internet marketing are not only growing, but they're exponentially adding more locations and employees.

CHAPTER 11: ————————————

OFFER A FIVE-STAR EXPERIENCE

"A hero is someone who has given his or her life to something bigger than oneself."

Joseph Campbell

Simply put, your personal training and the experience you provide to clients has to stand out. This does not necessarily mean that you have to have some unique equipment, which, of course, is also great and a nice way to draw attention like we do. But in addition to our high-tech training invention, we have also developed a focus on five-star service, results, and marketing. Clients come for service and results and you have to have it. If they get great service but not results, your clients will leave. If they get results but you have terrible customer service, they will also be likely to leave.

All of this means that you have to plan for success. Plan for your business' success and for your clients' success. If you don't offer top-notch training as well as the exceptional service and results that clients expect, your gym probably won't do very well or last very long.

Just as your clients need to learn to analyze food, calories, fat, protein, carbs, BMI, inches and more, your business needs to measure its focus and progress. You have to analyze cash flow, sales, expenses, receivables, appreciations, dues, increases and decreases in activity, the efficiency of your assets, employees and so much more. It all comes down to offering five-star personal training and all of the elements that go along with it. Plan for your success and ensure that everyone who works for you understands what it takes.

I am a big fan of Apple's plan for an exceptional experience:

Approach customers with a personalized warm welcome
Probe politely to understand all the customer's needs
Present a solution for the customers to take home
Listen for and resolve any issues or concerns
End with a fond farewell and an invitation to return.

The above spells APPLE and it is not a mistake. It is their checklist. You should use something like this for all your trainers as well. It is the perfect exploration of a good consultation. Did you know that Apple draws in more people in 90 days than Disney's four major theme parks in a whole year?

A big mistake that many personal trainers make is droning on about themselves and the business. Do you know what your clients love to talk about the most? Themselves! That's right. Ask questions to get them talking; you will learn more about the people you see every week and uncover potential business as well.

You should have a least 10 questions ready that will help you learn everything you need and want to know about your clients: all of their problems, why they are at your studio, why now and what would it mean to them if they finally reached their goal. Once you know everything about your client, including job, marital status, kids and other salient details, you can use all of that information to provide a solution for each one of your clients' concerns and problems. Yes, each one of them! This will develop greater trust and an even better relationship.

Never say that you are an expert, just call yourself a fitness professional or, even better, a personal trainer. When you say that you are expert, you create an imbalance in the relationship with your clients. And your client automatically questions your authority and, more than likely, you will be blamed if they don't get the exact results they want and expect. Use your pitch instead. Play it down and steal the show at the end.

One on one: connect with your clients

At our gym, we advocate for one-on-one training, service and relationships. Everyone else is doing group training now, the bigger, the better, because they are all about the money. However, you simply can't get the same results in a large group setting. Unless you are able to get all those people in, get their measurements such as weight, body fat, level of fitness, strength, and even if somehow you pull all this off, you still have to match every person with specific goals. Rather than providing inconsistent service in a harried atmosphere, we have decided to charge a premium; we don't do large groups and we guarantee results or we give their money back. It's not just about getting 10-20 people in a group and throwing some exercise at them. It's about creating connections, a culture of accountability and real results that can change people's lives. E-Fit, the effective and unique workout that we have developed and offer at our studios that includes full-body electrical muscle stimulation, gives us the chance to see two or three clients per trainer per hour and clients get amazing service and amazing results.

A five-star experience with exceptional customer service and outstanding results has always been my focus, which is why I wanted to come up with a new way of working out that would save time and be more effective for our clients.

As the founder and CEO of the 4U Fitness Franchise, I watched E-Fit's successful launch and saw that it had staying power in Europe. In 2012, I introduced E-Fit to the United States, and I developed a U.S. model with E-Fit Hungary as well. We worked together to acquire a 510(k) clearance from the FDA. With this I created a high-tech, hybrid fitness studio franchise—the only one of its kind offering electrical muscle stimulation in the United States. We also have a line of equipment and supplements that we have branded. We manufacture everything in Europe. We also developed an app with E-Fit to make it easy to schedule appointments and send out reminders. The app also controls the EF-1280 machine and records data for each client (for example, what exercises were done, the strength of the current during each exercise, how many reps were completed and so on). This allows each client to review their ongoing progress and see the improvements along the way.

Our 4U Fitness clients enjoy the high-tech system. Users can view themselves on the screen in 3D, and actually see what they are doing to their bodies—how their muscles react to their movements by contracting and relaxing. It's like watching a scientific movie all about you and your body. E-Fit is the foundation of 4U Fitness and almost everyone can use it—people who want to lose weight, lose inches, get rid of cellulite, and/or tone their bodies, as well as athletes and others who want to switch up their workout routine. E-Fit can help everybody achieve these goals. However, it is important to note that a few groups of people should not use E-Fit, including pregnant and breastfeeding women, and people with pacemakers or heart problems. As noted, the scientifically based E-Fit workout program is designed to crank up the intensity of traditional workouts, and is customized to each client's needs. Electrodes target the major muscle groups simultaneously, including: pectoral muscles, latissimus dorsi muscles, bicep and triceps muscles, lower back section of abdominal muscles, gluteal muscles and quadriceps femoris muscles, hamstrings, and calf muscles. The suit that our clients wear stimulates the entire body, making the muscles repeatedly contract and relax during the entire workout. This stimulation of 350 muscles, combined with active exercising, makes the workout as intense as possible and the results as outstanding as possible.

Every E-Fit session is 20 minutes long, and guided by a personal trainer, who controls and adjusts the intensity of the electrical currents. While wearing the suit, the user performs sets of exercises determined by the trainer, including push-ups, lunges, squats, and more. Trainers can add more electrodes, depending on the user's needs, and they can also increase the strength of the electrical current to make the muscles work to their maximum capability. They can also decrease the amount of stimulation during each exercise, making E-Fit a low-impact, easy-on-the-joints workout, with no weights required (for more advanced users, a workout with weights is more common). The trainer uses the app to control the session, which records data from the workout. These records then help the trainer decide how to adjust the user's sessions from week to week. Because the workout is so intense, the recommended frequency is just two, 20-minute sessions per week. Advanced athletes can withstand three 20-minute sessions in a week. Even with a necessary 48-hour rest period between each E-Fit session, the regimen can easily fit into most users' schedules—especially when you compare it to the traditional training period of 60 or 90 minutes daily. E-Fit provides intense, efficient, high-tech workouts that are great for almost everyone and every body.

A lot of users with back pain notice a reduction in pain after working out with E-Fit. Our clients work and strengthen all of these muscles, but without the heavy lifting. In addition, fat burning is an indirect benefit of EMS training. The expedited process allows the fat-burning process to begin sooner in the workout because the muscles are working harder than in a traditional workout. A low setting on the E-Fit machine increases the blood circulation and stimulates the tissue holding the fat, burning even more cellulite.

Why use E-Fit?

The full-body EMS EF-1280 workout system is highly efficient, enabling our clients to reach their fitness goals in a safe and timely manner. The EMS technology provides the equivalent of about a three-hour workout in just 20 minutes. During the training session, the device works 350 different muscles, contracting them a total of 36,000 times—that alone tells you how intense a workout it is. While it takes, on average, four sessions to see results, research has proven that working out with E-Fit is 18 times more effective than traditional personal training.

A study at German Sport University Cologne compared traditional strength training methods to full-body EMS training in order to assess the impact on an athlete's strength and speed. The researchers concluded that: "Dynamic full body EMS training... proved to be a highly effective means of increasing strength and speed as compared to other training methods"[1].

J. Vatter at Universität Bayreuth, located in Bayreuth, Germany, conducted a field study on the impact of full-body EMS training on a group of 134 people, both male and female. The subjects performed a full-body EMS workout twice a week for 12 weeks, dropping their body fat by an average of 1.4 percent. Eighty-two percent of participants noted that they'd gained relief from back pain as well[2].

---

1 Speicher, U, Nowak, S, Schmithüsen, J, Kleinöder, H, Mester. Long- and short- term training results through mechanical and Electro Muscle Stimulation (EMS) based on strength parameters. German Sport University Cologne 2008; published inter alia in BISp yearbook– research publication 2008/09.
2 Vatter, J. Electro Muscle Stimulation (EMS) as a full body training – Multi-fitness centre study. Universität Bayreuth, 2003; Publication AVM-Verlag München 2010.

Research by Mohd Faridz Ahmad and Amirul Hakim Hasbullah from the Universiti Teknologi MARA in Malaysia focused on using EMS to build male skeletal muscle mass. The results of the study found that "[Using an EMS to increase skeletal muscle mass is] beneficial to all human beings that in searched [sic] for healthy lifestyle and also good for athletes"[3].

As I've noted, there are multiple benefits of E-Fit personal training, including:

- Quick workouts
- Builds muscles
- Trains large muscle groups simultaneously
- Protects joints
- Burns fat
- Improves the appearance of cellulite
- Reduces back pain
- Features personal training
- Suitable for all ages, regardless of fitness level

That shows that the system is excellent, but that does not mean that it is fool-proof. There are thousands of studios worldwide using this technology now and they open and close just like any other business. They have good and bad reviews. Why? Because, ultimately, it is all about the people who operate these businesses and the service that they provide! You can have the best and the most advanced equipment but if you don't have the best people and systems in line to operate it, then it doesn't really matter. You can't save a business with just equipment. You need a system and service, not another certification or

---

3 Ahmad, MF, and Hasbullah, AH. The Effects of Electrical Muscle Stimulation (EMS) towards Male Skeletal Muscle Mass. International Journal of Medical, Health, Biomedical, Bioengineering and Pharmaceutical Engineering. 2015; 9(12):860-869.

another piece of fitness equipment! Think if this machine as a modern squat rack. Would that save your failing business? It might generate some buzz, but if you can't back it up the buzz, it will eventually die off and generate unhappy customers. This, in turn, will lead to some bad reviews and those bad reviews will eventually become bad debt.

In addition to that, being the only one and new is not always good. Did you see what Tesla went through recently? Being new and original is great if you are ready for the market, if you have great service and great systems in place. But not every company is ready to handle doubters and uncertainty.

CHAPTER 12: ———————

NUTRITION IS JUST AS IMPORTANT AS EXERCISE

"Just because you are not sick doesn't mean you are healthy."

unknown

When we talk about fitness, most people think about exercising, working out, training – which is obviously important. But nutrition is just as important. Every single personal training studio or big box gym has to have a nutritionist or a solid referral program to a nutritionist. When I say nutritionist, I don't mean any old dietitian. Your nutritionist has to be in alignment with your company's culture, mission and goals. Otherwise, this relationship can actually make everything worse! We simply cannot have a client on diet pills, fat burners or supplemental shakes doing a crash diet while you work them out in our studio doing a 20-minute workout that is the equivalent of three hours of exercise. If you did this, our clients would be passing out left and right, and they would end up losing more muscle than anything else. Clients can and do lose weight with shady supplements and diet pills, but they can't keep the weight off this way and it leads to a very unhealthy lifestyle. At our studios, we focus on healthy nutrition for the long term in addition to exercise. Make it a priority to find a nutritionist who can work with your clients and with your company's goals!

When you are trying to find the right nutritionist or nutritionists for your team, make sure you take the time to interview them and ask the right questions. Only together can you create the perfect plan that will help your clients get the results and benefit in the long run. It should never be about a quick fix or a crash diet! A full lifestyle change should be your goal and your clients need the guidance and education to execute that change successfully.

About 90% of the people who come into our studio try to cut out too much food initially, so that they are just eating salads. Combine this with intense exercise and you have a recipe for disaster. When you start working out, you actually have to start eating more, and many clients have been under eating to begin with. The problem is that many people try to follow a magazine diet, which is pretty ridiculous since every person's body is different, from metabolism to activity levels and more. We have hundreds and hundreds of clients but not a single client who has the same eating routine! It must be customized by a knowledgeable nutritionist. However, every three months or so, these magazines come out with the newest diet that they swear will work for millions of people, which if you ask me, should be illegal to do. Instead of offering a one-size-fits-all approach to diet and exercise, you can work with a smart nutritionist to give each client exactly what he or she needs to succeed. Each body will respond differently, something that these magazine diets fail to address. You have the opportunity to fix this! You need to educate your clients about how nutrition really works or they will get nowhere, even if they are exercising regularly. Or, if you do get some great results in the short term, it would be more from luck than anything else. You have to analyze and customize nutrition programs to really help your clients get the results they are looking for, and this requires a professional in nutrition.

Spend the time to learn more about this topic. Then find the right nutritionist who will take the time to actually teach your clients how to make meaningful changes instead of selling them on a dream.

CHAPTER 13:————————————

MIND OVER MATTER

"The future belongs to those who believe in the beauty
of their dreams."

Eleanor Roosevelt

The mind is very powerful. You probably know this already, but it
really becomes clear when it comes to working out.

Believe it or not, the mind is the most important part of working out!
It's all about the mind-body connection. When you realize what an
effect your mind has on your body, it only makes sense to use it to
your advantage. This is one of the reasons that our clients experience
impressive results – they believe in us, but, more importantly, they
believe in themselves. They believe that they will get the results that
they want and can already picture themselves and their results, thanks
to the mind-body connection.

According to a "New York Times" article called "Placebo Proves So
Powerful Even Experts are Surprised," a simple change in mindset can
make someone believe that they are taking an actual drug such that
their objective symptoms actually disappear.

In a Japanese research study, subjects were blindfolded and told their right arm was being rubbed with the poison ivy plant. Afterward, most of the 13 of the subjects' arms reacted to the classic symptoms of poison ivy, such as itching, boils and redness. This wouldn't be surprising, however, the actual plant used in the study was NOT poison ivy at all, just a harmless shrub. The subjects' beliefs were actually strong enough to create the biological effects of poison ivy, even though no such plant had ever touched their arms.

In another experiment, the researchers rubbed the subjects' other arm with actual poison ivy, but told them it was a harmless plant. Even though 13 students were highly allergic, only four of them broke out into the typical poison ivy rash[1].

It is clear that the brain is organized to act on what we predict will happen next. Dr. Marcel Kinsbourbe, a Neuroscientist at the New York School for Social Research, explains that our expectations create brain patterns that can be just as real as those created by the real world. In other words, a perceived event can trigger the same complex set of neurons to fire as though the event were actually taking place, triggering cascade events in the nervous system that will lead to a whole host of real physical consequences.

This same phenomenon has been proven by many other scientific studies. In one study a team performed an experiment on the cleaning staff of seven different hotels. They told half of the employees how much exercise they were getting every day simply by doing their work, how many calories their daily activities burned, how similar vacuuming is to a cardio workout and so on. The other half of the cleaning staff, as the control group, was given no such good news.

At the end of the experiment, several weeks later, the researchers

---

1 Blakeslee, S. (1998, October 13). Placebos prove so powerful even experts are surprised; new studies explore the brain's triumph over reality. Science. Retrieved from http://www.nytimes.com/1998/10/13/science/placebos-prove-so-powerful-even-experts-are-surprised-new-studies-explore-brain.html

found that those who had been primed to think of their work as exercise had actually lost weight, and their cholesterol levels dropped as well. These individuals had not done any additional work, nor had they exercised any more than control group. The only difference was in how their brains conceived of the work they were doing. That point is so important, it bears repeating: the mental construction of our daily activities, more than activities itself, defines our reality [2].

Believe in yourself, believe in your staff, believe in your mission

As a gym owner, you have to believe completely in what you and your staff are doing every day. You are changing people's lives. You have to love what you do and motivate your clients. You have to make your clients believe that this works and they will lose weight. You have to make sure they get it. As you can see, the mind is very, very strong. If you don't believe in EMS and start saying to clients that it's a great workout but you should do something else, add in some more cardio or whatever, they will believe that they should do other things to lose weight or build muscle. However, our clients who truly believe in us and in themselves and the workout get much better results in less time! We have many clients who have lost every pound they wanted to shed in the time frame they wanted because they believed in themselves. Likewise, we have had many clients who did the same with muscle building. Obviously, this has to be a realistic goal, but when that is set, anything is possible.

It is your job to sell your clients on their goal and dream and to teach them what is possible. When everyone believes, everyone succeeds. This is one of the reasons why some clients gain weight back so quickly.

---

2 Spiegel, A. (2008, January 3). Hotel maids challenge the placebo effect. Retrieved January 27, 2017, from http://www.npr.org/templates/story/story.php?storyId=17792517

Imagine this scenario: they have been eating clean but decide to meet some friends for drinks, bad food and maybe some dessert. What is the first thing they say when they see you next? They say, "I screwed up!" Or maybe "I cheated and I can feel the weight I already gained from it!" What is crazy is that they believe so strongly that they've put back on all the weight they've lost based on one cheat meal that eventually, it becomes a reality. And then the cycle continues – they blame weight gain on genetics, having a certain body type, you name it. But they are wrong, and it is your job to teach them otherwise. Don't just teach though, lead them and show them the way. Their new amazing life is in your hands!

We already have the latest technology in fitness and the most amazing personal trainers who can help our clients achieve incredible results. Just imagine if we focus on the mind as well! Since I have started to experiment with this, I have seen many impressive changes in clients who believed for so long they couldn't lose the weight. And all of a sudden, they did!

Make sure that your gym creates a culture that includes the mind-body connection. It's never just about lifting weights or doing cardio. It's about believing in yourself and the work that you're doing – knowing that you can achieve your dreams. We teach our clients that their dream can become a reality and we will show them how to reach it!

On that same note, your gym should also be a positive place, where positivity and motivation are key attributes in each member of your staff. Research has proven that just thinking positively will boost your endorphin levels by 27%. How amazing is that? In fact, when we are happy or even watching a happy cat video (if you are a cat person, of course), we can perform better. A study at Harvard University involved two groups of students who were given the same math test[3]. One group

---

3 Achor, S. (2012, January 1). Positive intelligence. Retrieved January 27, 2017, from Productivity, https://hbr.org/2012/01/positive-intelligence

watched funny videos and joked around before the test while the other group just took the test. Guess who did better? The group who was relaxed and having fun ahead of time outperformed the other group by 52 %. Most people believe that success precedes happiness. Once they reach their goal, such as a promotion at work, losing a certain amount of weight or gaining a certain percentage of muscle, then they will feel great and be happy. But that isn't how it works. You have to believe in yourself first – success comes much easier to happy people who believe in their own dreams.

The power of positivity cannot truly be defined because ultimately, the power is endless. Whether it is in your personal or professional life, your mentality can completely change the direction and outcome. Shawn Achor knows the connection between happiness and success. He says "People who cultivate a positive mind-set perform better in the face of challenge," and calls it the "happiness advantage—every business outcome shows improvement when the brain is positive." Of course happiness can be defined differently to each person but the definition of positivity would be the same. From 225 academic studies, statistical analysis was done forming a meta-analysis that allowed researchers Sonja Lyubomirsky, Laura King, and Ed Diener to find striking evidence of a direct causality between life satisfaction and successful business outcomes.

If your gym or personal training studio is full of happy people who know how to motivate their clients, you will be a success. It's mind over matter. We recently added a client journal to give our clients the chance to set goals, track their results and stay on track. It's positive reinforcement. We encourage them to read through their goals every night before they go to sleep and believe in themselves. The clients who adopt this simple daily habit get better results than the clients who don't set and track their goals.

CHAPTER 14:

MAKE THE RIGHT HIRING DECISIONS

"Talent wins games, but teamwork and intelligence win championships."

Michael Jordan

I have mentioned before that you need to have the right people with the right attitude in order to motivate clients and keep them coming back and to create a five-star experience in your gym. I always encourage gym owners to hire based on attitude and not on paper qualifications. I personally never ask my trainers to show me their certifications during the interview process.

Generally, they want to talk about their master's degree in exercise science and they should be proud of the time and effort they put in, but that doesn't influence my hiring decisions. If you are the right fit, you will be hired regardless of your education and certifications. Just because you have a diploma and some certifications doesn't mean you are a superstar personal trainer and vice versa.

What kind of people do you want to work with?

First, you have to identify what qualities you are looking for in your employees. Meaning, all employees from personal trainers to managers, even receptionists, think of every single person in your gym. You need to have specifics when you think about this, not out of an outdated job description booklet.

You should create a one-page document for every position which lists job title, mission, and expectations for the next three, six and 12 months. For example, you could include the following: generating $5,000 revenue monthly within three months of employment or have 20 active clients by the end of two months. You can also list activities such as: you will be required to make X amount of phone calls per day and to book three trials and seven sessions per week. Just be specific! And really ask yourself: can this person take my business to seven figures? Make sure that you also list job competencies and that your candidates align with them – this includes things like work ethic, willingness to learn, an upbeat personality, the ability to motivate others and so on. It is better to hire for a cultural and competency fit than for specific skills as long as they are capable of learning and you have to tools to teach them. In my case, when I hire someone it takes about three months to train them; in this time, they learn exactly what, why, when and how we do what we do. It is important that they are open minded because we teach them the truth about the fitness and health industry and sometimes the truth is tough to swallow. We show them why we are different and how we are going to revolutionize the fitness industry.

We show them how to think differently and their job is to show and teach the same to our clients as well. Training is a very important part of our culture. We even give our employee their own certifications and ID cards. Once they pass all of our exams, they receive a diploma and an ID card which they use to log into our systems, so every session is documented and every motion of the workout can be analyzed in our cloud-based system.

If someone doesn't fit in with your culture, it simply won't work – even worse, a bad hire can damage your culture and hurt your business.

So how do you get you're A-team? How do you attract and keep the most amazing trainers for your business?

I will share some of our top tips and secrets here – just keep an open mind, because we do things a little differently – and you might even think some of these ideas are a little crazy. But they work!

Find at least 20 candidates per job opening

Statistics show that you need at least 20 candidates to find one good hire. Sadly, many gym owners hire the first person who walks in their gym soley based on if they look the part. That is a recipe for disaster. For instance, sometimes you grow too fast and you need to find a trainer as soon as possible, or one of your trainers leaves and you are stressed out about finding a new one so you hire the first candidate that seems good enough. Please do not do this. I did it one time and had a horrible experience; our business ended up losing thousands of dollars because clients left and, on top of that, we lost thousands of potential dollars because these people started to talk about our trainer and what was happening. It took us about six months to recover from that bad hire. I can only blame myself since I was the one who hired the person. When I did not have a hiring process and didn't know who I was really looking for, my trainer retention was horrible. They would only stay about three to six months and I had to fire them or they fired themselves. Once I created our process and figured out what I need to secure our company's future and who I need to fill up each one of these roles, everything changed. Now we don't hire for a job anymore. We hire for a career, a calling! Yes, we are saving the dolphins at 4U Fitness and you should, too. Our trainers are part of our family and they are not here just to collect a paycheck. They are contributing to our future and, most importantly, they believe in our business and they know where we heading and have no reason to leave. Most of our trainers been with us for years now and we just keep adding new ones as we grow while retaining the best in the business.

You have to have a documented hiring process and be willing to look at lots of applicants.

I have learned from Google because they have used some very creative ways to find new talent. In 2004 they placed a billboard by a busy highway next to Yahoo's headquarters. They put a mathematical riddle on the billboard – it didn't include any mention of Google, its logo or any type of branding. No one knew who did it, until someone cracked the riddle. It generated a huge amount of media requests and posts as well as increased interest in this competitor to Yahoo.

The billboard read "{first 10-digit prime found in consecutive digits e}.com" The answer 7427466391.com would to a website with another equation to solve, with no sign of branding or any trace of Google.

If someone solved this equation it would lead to a page on Google Lab which read: "One thing we learned while building Google is that it's easier to find what you're looking for if it comes looking for you. What we are looking for are the best engineers in the world. And here you are. "

Now THAT is creative hiring. Not to mention it will only attract the people they were actually looking for – not just smart and skilled in math/engineering but the ones who willing to do the extra work and to figure out things on their own. Like Google, we don't want someone who will just sit there and look at you if something breaks or the music system in your studio isn't working. We want someone who will take charge and figure it out.

What do we do to stand out? We used social media to post funny and goofy pictures of our trainers with a title like: Are you an entrepreneur stuck in a personal trainer's body? Would you rather work for David or

Goliath? We also have pictures of our trainers in lab coats and glasses standing around Miss Olympia, who is in the middle wearing our workout equipment with a caption of "4U Fitness where science meet fitness." We aren't afraid to have fun.

At fitness expos and conferences, we give out black envelopes to personal trainers that we really like. These envelopes have nothing on them; they are just very heavy thick and feel expensive in your hand. When they open it, they see a specific time and place to meet for an interview. When they show up, they see that there are other trainers there as well but we like to keep it to only about three to five personal trainers; in this way, we let them know that they are the elite of the elite. We were like a trendy coffee shop or bar like a speakeasy where you have to know the answer to get in. If you can find a place nearby that requires you to know the password to get in, that ads extra credit to this process. Once they arrive for the interview we ask as many questions needed to find out as much as possible and give out very minimal information to keep them interested. Being very secretive in a FBI style meeting is a cool experience. After this process, we leave and we don't have to do anything since the good candidate will definitely follow up with you.

Luckily, we also receive many job inquiries monthly. We even have personal trainers who fill out our free trial form to get an inside view on our studio; this often leads to them following up by asking for a job. I have a collection of resumes on my desk as well, since we receive several each week; we aren't hiring now, but I do save these for future hiring sprees.

Once you have the right hiring system in place, you should attract at least 20 candidates per job post. You will have to narrow them down to the final three, which should be easy if you have the right system. Once you reach to the final three candidates, then it is time to get down to the details!

Here is how our process works at this point:

1. Once you have several good candidates to meet with, it is time for the screening. Set some rules and make sure you are ready.

2. I set the rules in job postings and I write down exactly what I want them to do. For example, I might ask a personal trainer to send me a resume and cover letter to 4U Fitness, explaining why we should read the resume. I tell them to send it to this email address and do not call us. I also state that if we pick you, you will hear from us in two weeks.

3. If people just send me a resume, then they go in the discard pile. It doesn't matter how good the resume is – if you can't follow the rules, then you are not getting hired.

4. If they send their resume and cover letter but it is not directed to me or 4U Fitness, I also hit the delete button. That means they didn't even take the time to update one. They are just hitting copy and paste.

5. If they email the wrong email address, I won't even open it. If they call my receptionist, he or she would tell them to follow the instructions which clearly states no phone calls. So whoever calls us is not getting hired.

6. While following-up does show initiative, if they start calling or emailing again within the two weeks I mentioned, it shows that they can't follow instructions. This is really important.

7. Once we successfully get to the next stage, I will pass on the resumes/cover letters that I like to my personal trainers, who will then set up a four-step interview process. I recommend that you let your employees also meet the new candidate for evaluation. We have a system that rates all these candidates and if one of the candidates receives two or more B's, they won't be hired, no matter what. It shows that I trust and value my employees.

8. Next, three of my trainers meet with the future candidates for

a formal interviewing, asking a variety of questions and then grade them while the candidate gets homework. If the candidate chooses not to complete this homework, they will not be hired. Once homework is completed, they have the final step, which is writing a 1,000-word essay to me about why we should hire them and why are they the best fit for us. Once I read that essay, I decide whether to meet them.

9. Always hire less and pay them more! There are so many companies who hire fewer people and pay them more than the industry average; this way they attract the right people to their business and they are able to keep them. On top of that, these businesses also save money because their employees are more productive and they also have a very low employee turnover rate!

"While in a big company one bad hire is an issue, In a start-up it can spell the difference between success and failure!."

Unknown

Success lies in the hands of your trainers and staff

These individuals will be representing your business and brand on a daily basis. They are the face of your product. That is why it is of the upmost importance that an in-depth interview process be completed. This outline explains our interview process in greater detail.

Interview process:

a. 1st interview: Candidate meets one of our trainers. (Facetime or Skype if the individual lives out of town/state)

b.   2nd interview: with another staff member

c.   3nd interview: Candidate meets the staff and is shown their future working environment

d.   After the candidate has been chosen to move forward with the process, they will be issued a take-home assignment.

e.   After the completed home assignment, they are required to write the 1,000-word essay about why they should be hired.

f.   The last step is the meeting and interview with me.

Take-Home Assignment: Each candidate will be given three questions (see below).

Upon the next scheduled meeting, candidates present their responses. Assemble your personal trainers who have been helping with the interviews and let them know that they should makes notes during candidate presentations.

Candidates can present their responses in any format they choose (i.e., written, verbally, on a display board or in a PowerPoint presentation). There should be no set requirement for presentations.

During this in-person session, the top candidates will separate themselves from the pack. Top candidates will go above and beyond to show you their creative abilities. Remember, detailed presentations are not required, but we hope for the best and most creative! We are not looking for the right answers but rather how they think and where their focus lies!

- **Question #1 - Strategic:**

    Example: How do you plan on growing your clientele base?

- **Question #2 - Tactical:**

    Example: How would you overcome an overwhelming number of clients? If availability is limited and spots are getting tight, what would be your solution?"

- **Questions #3 - Unconventional/Creativity:**

  Example: How would you make your work environment engaging and enjoyable for your staff and clientele?

  Example: What would you do to ensure your business will stand out from the crowd? Specifically, how will you thrive against the stereotypical chain competitors?

  If the punishment for parking on double yellow lines were death, and therefore nobody did it, would that be a just and effective law? (They are not meant to give a right or wrong answer here. They need to demonstrate that they have recognized the various issues that arise. The answer to its effectiveness is already in question)

These questions and their responses are the most important. At this point, a candidate should demonstrate his or her passion in what they believe in. What are their boundaries? Do they think "outside of the box"?

Extra credit: Ask your candidates to come up with their own title that signifies their persona.

This title should encompass their attitude and the uniqueness of who they are and who they want to be. This title demonstrates the flexibility that they will have at 4U Fitness, along with their ability to be inventive.

Example: A former candidate dubbed himself as "Sales Master." This name speaks volumes, especially if he lives up to his name. Unfortunately, it turned out that "sales" was actually his weakness and not his strength, but we liked the name and creativity.

Candidate observations: What to look for throughout the hiring process and during presentations

a. Does the candidate seem well-prepared and confident?

b. Are they interested in selling themselves or are they here to contribute to our core values and team?

c. How do they respond to instruction and constructive criticism?

d. Are they receptive to the idea of learning new training styles and methods?

e. Do they demonstrate a friendly and outgoing personality?

f. Do they demonstrate a true passion for helping others?

g. Are they willing to go above and beyond their "job description"?

h. Do they appear to be a creative thinker?

i. Would they stand out in a crowd?

j. Do they seem to be well-rounded and versatile in their strengths?

k. Do they fit in to our culture?

l. Do they have the ambition and drive to establish a career with 4U Fitness?

Check for culture and creativity.

Depending on your business, you will want to customize your questions to your culture.

We adapted a great question from a company called MOMs. Since we need open- minded people, we need to ask the right questions and MOMs share some of their questions in the book of "Scaling Up" by Verne Harnish. For example, we ask our potential candidates, "Do you discuss politics, religion or fitness beliefs with people?" "When was your last passionate debate?" "Who was it with? And what was it about? How did it turn out?" If they say that they will never respect the person they debated again, we know it is not the right person to hire since he or she is not open minded.

MOMs has a great system for hiring. A few great examples of what they ask are "What did you spend money on as a teenager and where did you get this money from?" You will definitely not impress a MOM's team member by saying by your parents gave it to you.

We also like to ask creative questions to see how potential candidates solve problems. For example: How many gas stations are in the United States? Obviously, we are not looking for the correct answer. We are looking for creativity and to see how they solve problems, how they try to figure out things. If they simply say, "I don't know" and give up, then they are not the right person for you.

One of my favorite creative questions to ask is also used by Apple in its interviewing process: You have 100 coins lying flat on a table, each with a head side and a tail side: 10 of them are heads up, 90 are tails up. You can't feel, see or in any other way find out which side is up. Split the coins into two piles such that there are the same numbers of heads in each pile. How do you do that? Just think about it. If you can't figure it out, you can read the answer later in this book.

The answer to the 100 coins again involves creative thinking and how to solve a problem. But it simple. You divide them into two piles with 50 coins each and that is it. There are an equal number of heads in each pile. Since we never asked you to have them facing up or anything, you will have two equal piles of heads simply by having two equal piles of coins!

Another creative approach is held by online apparel retailer Zappos; during their process, they ask a lower level employee to interview the potential candidate. If the candidate gets irritated by this, then he or she probably lacks one of Zappos' core values, which is being humble. It also gives that employee a chance to contribute and shine.

If you want to read a little more about our hiring process, we have been featured in several blogs and magazines; you can check out this one: http://www.jobvite.com/blog/anatomy-perfect-new-hire/

It is most important to remember to use your core values during your hiring process! This way you can always determine if someone fits in with your culture or not. Later on in the hiring process, you can ask job candidates to talk more about what values resonated with them. If they are not as interested in our core values or they don't feel motivated by this process, then they are not a good hire.

Hire your weaknesses first

Not every gym owner thinks about doing this, but you will build a stronger team when you hire your weaknesses first. If you are already good at most things, you need to cover that area where you aren't as strong. For example, if you are bad with numbers, hire an accountant! If no one on your team speaks Spanish but you have many clients who do, focus on hiring someone who speaks several languages.

Only hire A+ players and let your current players know that they are all A+ players and this company won't hire B players. Build your team up and remind them of their strengths throughout the hiring process.

Bring out the welcome mat

Once they're hired, it's time to celebrate these candidates! Have a welcome party! They should feel really special and that they have made the right decision. This will help every new hire become a raving fan of your business! At 4U Fitness, all of our new hires receive a special 4U Fitness cheesecake and a relaxing day at a local spa; we even pay for a friend/partner/spouse to join them.

Even while you're celebrating this new hire, you have to think of this as a test period; this is why we first give all of our new hires a 90-day contract to start. At the end of the contract period, we use a thorough evaluation process to make our ultimate hiring decision. If they meet everything on the list, they will be hired. If they don't, they will either leave (on their own or at our decision) or they can focus on continual improvement until they are hired as a full employee.

Once you have all agreed that this is a great fit, it is important to remember that you must invest in their ongoing education and culture.

At 4U Fitness each trainer is required to spend at least 12 hours of continued education at our 4U Fitness University to able to renew their certification with us. When we hire someone, we move them though our schooling system and we give them an actual graduation and they receive an ID card and diploma, which they have to renew each year.

In addition to general training, your new hires must learn more about your company culture and core values. If you operate a relatively small company, then your new employees will learn from this information from the start, just being around you and your team. I do not recommend handing new employees a long and overwhelming document to read and tell them they will find everything there. This is not inspirational and isn't a good way to teach culture.

Make sure that core values and culture are a part of everything that you do. This includes your employee handbook, ongoing training and even meetings with your staff. When you have brief meetings with your trainers, make sure that you refer back to all of your core values in anything that they do that is good or bad.

In addition, all of your new hires should get a full walk-through and tour and sit down to talk with everyone on your staff. Everyone can share your core values and goals of the business and what it stands for. What does the future looks like for the company? Where did you start from? What is your story? Why did you do this? What does it mean to you? And where does your new employee fit into all of this? What is his or her role in the company and the message that he or she needs to deliver?

This is the good time to start with their personal pitch. Yes, as we discussed earlier, all of your employees, even the receptionist, needs to have their own pitch. Have your new employee introduce him or herself and explain why they came to you and is doing this in their life. Find out what this job means and how this company can play a part in her goals.

During the introduction and getting to know each other process, ask your employees to share their pitches with the new employee – and watch to see what the new employee's reaction is in return. This experience will likely blow this new hire away! To be honest with you, I have yet to meet a gym or a personal trainer who has this part down right. Everyone thinks they know what they are doing and why they are special but every time I go into a gym and I ask that gym's personal trainers what their company does, every single one of them will say something different. Something like: getting people fit, all about fat loss, personal training or whatever. No, they need to know what the company stands for, why they are here and why they are doing this. It all should be a consistent message. The only thing that should be different is each person's title and the reason WHY they are in this business. That's it. The rest should be exactly the same. By introducing your new hire to the company culture early, it will make a huge difference. Have the new hire spend time with your personal trainers. Shadow them all the time before you let her train anyone (or answer the phones or handle the books). Then have your new hire train you and all your trainers until you are all happy with her. Always give honest feedback, otherwise they won't be able to improve!

Culture, culture and more culture

Culture is the most important aspect for a business. Without culture, you cannot grow a business successfully. At 4U Fitness, we host a monthly event that everyone looks forward to – sometimes I don't even tell them what is coming to create a greater sense of excitement. I will remind them at the beginning of the month that this month on Friday the 16th we are meeting at our Tampa location at 5:59 p.m. sharp and we are getting on to a bus and departing to Orlando by 6:01 p.m. No more details. I let their imagination do the rest. I will be asked every single day what we are going to do; I will receive texts and emails and I honestly can hear and feel their excitement. I give them little hints but make it impossible to figure out. I even had someone email me with a detailed list of events in Orlando around that time frame that he thinks we are doing because it fits into our culture. Well, he was wrong. We are doing something way different this time. Just to show my appreciation and have a fun bonding time traveling to Orlando all together to have some fun, reinforce our culture and build an even stronger team.

One other thing that we want to do together is to go volunteer one day each month. With all my trainers at each staff meeting, we will sit down and pick a nonprofit and we will go donate our time to help that nonprofit out for a whole day. For example, the first location we chose was the Humane Society of Tampa Bay. Who doesn't love animals? I really want to build the giving back aspect into our culture. I want to give back to the community. That is what 4U Fitness is about. Helping people and giving back.

Lead with trust

"While in a big company one bad hire is an issue,
In a start-up it can spell the difference between success
and failure!."

Unknown

Letting go and trusting your hires to do things good is one of the hardest thing to do as a business leader in a new and growing company. Most personal trainers who have their own businesses prefer to operate alone. The only way to do this is to hire for your weaknesses and then delegate those items to the first personal trainers you hire; this will show them that you trust them and it will show you that you made the right hires. Whether it is training, group classes, sales, consultation, marketing, accounting or something else, you have to let go and trust your team in order to be successful. Than the next step will be to hire and train trainers to repeat your process and clone your amazing services. It all should be the same since it is systematized. You cannot hire a trainer and just let them do what they want. That is a recipe for disaster.

The most successful business leaders have a clear vision and solid routines in place in order to make their goals a reality. Goals without routines are useless, just like routines without goals are not going to work either. I had my goals and routines set to achieve my dream: I even had exact dates to reach my deadlines including getting into "Entrepreneur" magazine before my 28th birthday. One day before my birthday, on December 3, I received my copy of "Entrepreneur" magazine in the mail and it was one of the best feelings in the world to open it up and see a picture of our gym and staff and to read about myself in a magazine that I believe in. And on top of that, I reached my goal one day before I turned 28. What an awesome accomplishment and gift to myself!

Without a clear vision for your business as well as established business goals and requirements for your employees or contractors, you can't steer the ship. In fact, it might turn into more of a Titanic situation than a Love Boat scenario.

You also have to let all of your trainers know what you expect from them. Have a clear employee handbook with a clear contract which will explain the compensation plan, bonuses, sick pay, penalties and, most importantly, your expectations as their leader.

When you hire your first trainer, the following steps can help smooth the process out:

1. Give them your handbook if you have one already (if not, you need to write one with your hire and continuously ask for feedback to ensure that you have everything covered).
2. Teach them the pitch, company mission and your system.

3. Pinpoint what this trainer needs to accomplish.

4. Measure for success - create a system that allows you to measure performance.

5. Always give feedback to your trainer on how he or she is doing.

6. Don't be shy about saying thank you - give your trainer recognition for their accomplishments and reward them when it's deserved.

7. There is nothing so unequal as the equal treatment of unequals - think about this and use it! Do not treat everyone the same. A great leader adjusts his or her leadership style to the situation.

This is the easy part. After this comes the real leadership! If you used our hiring process or you have a good system and you were able to hire amazing trainers for the culture, then half of your job is already taken care of. But if you hired for looks, or some sort of voodoo or Jedi instincts or, even worse, you tried to hire yourself, you are heading to a really dark place soon. And, trust me, you will not be able to fix it. I thought I could fix bad situations and bad hires many times but I couldn't. In those cases, I should have cut my losses and then fixed my hiring process and moved on! Learn from my mistakes. However, it took me more than one bad hire before I finally realized I need to invest some time into the hiring process, which we just discussed in detail. Take care of the hiring and your employees will help you take care of your business' success.

CHAPTER 15: —————————

MANAGING A SUCCESSFUL PERSONAL TRAINING BUSINESS

"I learned that you don't get anywhere by sitting comfortably in a chair."

Conrad Hilton

Now that you have made some great hires, trained them on your culture and the importance of the pitch, and still have had some fun along the way, it is time to ensure that your overall management style is in line with your vision.

Following are several key management tips that will help you succeed:

- Inspire and coach people, don't just demand things of them. It is all about your people, it's not all about the numbers. Your numbers will take care of themselves as long as you take care of your team. The team must understand 100% how you do things and you need to be absolutely clear about the message they need to deliver. This is when your pitch also comes in very handy. Remember, you will get only what you pitch for!

- Don't be a seagull manager! Do not fly in and make a lot of noise by yelling at everyone, basically poop on them and then fly out. That is exactly how they will lose their motivation and start looking for another job while not performing their best at their current one. Do not look for negatives only, look for all the positives as well and recognize them. Bring them up and talk about them. You really need to look at everything. Don't be a seagull. Always celebrate success! Show your team that you appreciate them. Even if you only have small accomplishments to recognize at the beginning, make sure you celebrate them!

- Your important communications should be face to face communication. Not email, not text. Face to face. Don't forget to make notes on what you have talked about so you can bring proof and refer back if needed later on.

- Establish your culture! Define how you are going to treat your employees and what you expect from them. The most valuable asset you can have in your business is your people – not your equipment. Without the right culture and the right people, you have nothing.

- If you ever need to fire someone, do it right away, do not delay. It is never easy but the worst thing to do is drag it out. You will end up losing clients and will have a bad atmosphere in your gym in the meantime.

- Have weekly, monthly and quarterly staff meetings with goals and things to go over and work on. Make sure that someone creates a "who, what and when" list for each employee. Write it down after each meeting and keep them accountable for what they are going to do by when and who is responsible for what.

- Make employees take ownership of their own delivery dates. Don't say you have to do this by Friday at 2 p.m. If they set that deadline themselves, then they will be working hard for themselves. It's distinction that they can feel when they sign up to do their own work! Give employees the ability to make decisions and then stay accountable for those decisions.

- One of the worst things you can do as a business owner is to take your popularity over your accountability. If you have team member struggling to get results, not showing up on time, canceling clients, not delivering on the promised numbers and so on, make sure you take the right steps in leadership. Firstly, did you take the time to teach them enough? Did you give them clear goals and teach them how to accomplish those goals? Is this team member failing because of your lack of communication? Or is he or she just not delivering? Either way take the right steps: sit down with this person, warn them about potential consequences, remind and revisit goals. Take time to fix the situation; you might need to put your foot down and remind them that their job might be in jeopardy, even if they are 15 years older than you are. I highly recommend that you make it clear to your team that if they don't meet your expectations and if they don't perform, they will be gone. That is the bottom line. Tell your team members exactly what you expect from them and constantly remind them about those expectations. If they fail, make the consequences clear and if they cannot improve, they will have to leave. Sometimes that is a decision that must be made.

Keep one more thing in mind. If you are a personal trainer expert with no knowledge in marketing, and you hired a great marketing team but they don't meet your expectations, don't just fire them after a month. Keep reminding them of what you want, what you need and what you expect. Keep them accountable and make it very clear. It is not fair to fire someone because you failed to manage them and because you failed to keep them accountable. They might not even know what you need from them! Make it clear and don't be afraid of making someone upset or losing your popularity score. It's business, not personal!

My last piece of advice is to always challenge your ideas by using your team. Trust your team and get them involved in all of your decision making. Even if you already made a decision on something, it will be well worth it to have your team involved, even if it is something small like buying X branded weights over Y branded ones. By giving them a choice and part in the decision, you will create the greatest level of trust that you can possibly give them and they will return it with respect. Don't be scared about opening up to your team. Show them that you are also vulnerable and they will appreciate your displays of openness and honesty.

CHAPTER 16:————————

STAY ON TOP OF YOUR FINANCIALS

"The wise man puts all his eggs in one basket and watches the basket."

Andrew Carnegie

As we have discussed before, there are many great products and companies that don't make it and eventually go out of business. That is why you have to measure results and you have to know your numbers! Most gym owners think that getting more sales to increase revenue is the right way to start when it comes to financial figures. However, this is not the best option. The first thing you should do is sit down and take a look at your financial results, compare them month to month and year to year to see what you can adjust, reduce or cut. Ask yourself the question, "Does my business need this? Is this something that I need or want? What is the purpose of this expense? What is the return on it?" Everything can be measured to cut off the fat: simply by dropping 10% of your extra expenses, you can raise your revenue by 50%, if you run your business around 90% of expenses of your profits.

To get better cash flow, you need to receive more money on time and also pay your bills on the latest day possible. This way you get the cash from your clients on time and you don't need chase after them. In turn, you will have it in your business account longer, giving you time to make a wise investment before paying your bills on their due date. Every month, I pay the rent on each location on the absolute last day of my agreement.

Do not tolerate your clients not paying on time. Be clear. It is not worth the energy and time to chase after your money. I have had clients who would "forget their wallet" and then cancel at the last minute three times, and then get sick – then they don't want to pay. Or when they come in, they try to get away with it. This means that their receivable was delayed by at least a month. This scenario is not good for your cash flow and it is definitely not good to keep seeing these clients; it will add even more stress and problems down the road. It is not worth it. They know better and you can bet that they pay their other bills on time or they wouldn't have electricity or water to shower.

You need to learn how to manage your money. Do you think you will have less stress and more money in the bank if you earn more? No; unfortunately, that is actually a myth. People adjust their spending. If you have been making $40,000 a year and you start making $50,000, then you will likely end up with the same amount in the bank. That is why most lottery winners often go broke in just two to five years after they've won. This doesn't make sense but it does happen. You need to learn how to manage your money; if you have problems I highly recommend reading "The Richest Man in Babylon."

Once you have all of your financial matters in hand, then you can begin to work more on your sales process.

CHAPTER 17: ————————

SELL, SELL, SELL

Whether you are a personal trainer, manager, gym owner or anything else, you are also a salesperson. You sell every single day. You also sell to your parents, to your friends, to your spouse, to anyone you meet, you are continuously selling. Doesn't matter if you don't think about it or you aren't very good at it, you are still selling. With that in mind, it should be your number one goal is to be the best at selling or, as I mentioned earlier, if you don't know how to pitch or sell you will be sold on the people you talk to. And your wallet will be empty.

According to Patrick Bet-David, there are three different types of people in the world when you are prospecting: People you don't know, people you do know and people your people know. Which is absolutely correct. Obviously, the hardest to sell to is people you do not know. This is why you really need to know your pitch to grab their attention and then really focus on their problems; if you know you can help them with your product and services, it should be your number one goal to make the sale! If you don't, you are really hurting them and your business. Since you are absolutely sure that you have the solution for them, you need to figure out the way to really sell them on it. The problem that most people face is that they have an amazing product or service but they have no idea how to sell it. This is why so many businesses and products never make it, even if they are good, even if they are the best of the best! Because they don't know how to sell.

The problem that most people face is that they have an amazing product or service but they have no idea how to sell it. This is why so many businesses and products never make it, even if they are good, even if they are the best of the best! Because they don't know how to sell.

This is why I recommend the following five-step sales process.

1. Ask questions about your prospect, lots of questions, find out what they really need.
2. Based on those answers, link your business and services to their specific wants and needs.
3. Focus on a warm tone of voice, positive body language and common words or professional words.
4. Never let your prospect compare prices to someone else.
5. Use scarcity to close.

For the first two steps, ask questions! We have 20 questions to ask a new consult. You, too, should have a specific list designed to not only get all the information you need to figure out if this is a client you can truly help, but also to get the specifics out on how to sell this client on your services. Really get into the details about their goal. Ask them what their goal is. Ask them, "What would it really mean to you if you could reach your goal?" Tell them to really think about it and imagine themselves in the future achieving that goal. And then ask them to tell you what it felt like and what would it mean to them! Then ask their specific wants and needs, find out their previous history what they liked or didn't like about previous gyms or trainers, what is their job, are they limited on time, etc.

Once you know all the details you can really build an answer that you can sell them on. For example, let's say we have a prospect whose name is Nina. Nina is a busy mom who doesn't want to bulk up but does want to tone and get lean but she says she doesn't have any time to exercise. In response to Nina's problem, we would say something like this:

"That's great, Nina! Because we specialize in helping women just like you lean out and lose fat. We've developed a high-tech invention that is designed to transform women and tighten their skin, making the muscles stronger and the body leaner than ever. It is a three-hour workout that can be completed in just 20 minutes. And the heaviest weight you will ever touch is just two pounds."

In that short response, I gave Nina a solution to all of her issues! During the rest of the consolation with Nina, I will focus on reflecting back to these issues.

In step #3: Recognize your audience and make adjustments as needed. If you have a guy who comes in to a consultation with a really deep and loud voice who continuously tries to talk over you, you definitely have to step it up and talk over him to show who's boss. Otherwise he won't trust you and won't buy anything from you. However, when you have a person who is quiet and timid in personality and voice, you need to adjust to that as well. Otherwise you can scare that client away. All the while, you should be trying to pick up on their body language; if they sit with their legs crossed you do the same. If you try to reflect back similar their body language, tone of voice and the words they use, they will see themselves in you and they will leave with a good vibe, excited about doing business with you since you have so much in common.

In step #4: Never let your prospect compare your prices to someone else. Imagine this: a prospect walks in and all she wants to know is the price. We charge almost double the average in our area. What do you think she would do if we told her that? She would say, "Wow, that is way too expensive and you guys are crazy." You simply can't start with this information and allow her to do that. Right away you need to ask "Expensive? What do you mean? Why do you think we are expensive? Expensive to what? What do you compare us to?" You have to find out she's comparing you to the gym down the street who charges $10 per month for membership or if it's the personal trainer down the street who just opened so he discounted his prices to attract new customers and it will be out of business soon. Or is it all the personal training studios in the area who charge half of what you charge but train clients for an hour, three or four times per week without a fully detailed nutrition and workout plan with detailed analysis? In this case, it is like comparing a luxury car with a 1992 basic Honda. You just can't do that.

They need to know the value. In our case, we cut the workout in less than half and made it more effective where we also guarantee the results or we give their money back. This means that they have no risk whatsoever. And these are just the basics. But the point is nobody out there is quite like us so there is just no way to compare our prices to someone else. It is like comparing a heart surgeon to a dentist. How come a heart surgeon costs so much more than a dentist? They are both doctors, just like we are all gyms. But we have very different roles. In step #5: Now it's time to close the deal! If, for some reason, the prospective client is still not ready to close with you, it is time to scare them a little. For example, you can say something like "This is our limited time only price and we are raising our prices next month but if you sign up now you will be grandfathered in with our current rate forever." Or, "No problem I can follow up with you soon but I just want to let you know that I only have three spots remaining and I have five more consults this week with five lovely women who just had babies, but I can only take three so after that I would have to put you on the waiting list." When you start to paint a picture in their mind that other people just like them are signing up, this should definitely do the job.

If you want to learn more about our sales process and research methods, check this out: http://www.patrickbetdavid.com/sales-process/

CHAPTER 18:————————

KEEP 'EM COMING BACK FOR MORE

"A boomerang returns back to the person who throws it. But first, while moving in a circle, it hits its target."

Vera Nazarian

Now that you have new clients and members coming through the door, you have to focus on keeping them. The real work starts now! If you used all the tools I gave you so far, you should have no problem with keeping your clients. You have a great culture and an amazing team around to support it. It really comes down to your leadership. You have to have goals, as well as a system in place that the trainers follow in order to delight the clients. Every little detail counts. Actually, it is all about the little things! Our trainers text our clients every morning with a very creative and funny message to keep them motivated and accountable. On top of that, we have a full-time nutritionist who regularly checks on our clients through our app and via phone to make sure they are staying on top of their eating. She is coaching them through their everyday life. It's all about keeping them engaged. Our goal is to educate them and to teach them how it really works and that takes some time!

On time all the time

Your trainers should never, ever be late. If a personal trainer arrives 15 minutes before a session, then he or she is on time. At our studio, we consider 14 minutes early to be late. Even if the client says that they understand, they do care and eventually they will leave. You know why? Because it sends the wrong signal! They will start to think that they are in the way of your trainer since your trainer is so busy and they don't want to feel like an inconvenience. If that continues, the client eventually stop coming because no one wants to be in the way. On top of that, they will feel rushed because, when a trainer arrives after the client, it means the trainer has no time to prepare for the session. If the client feels even a little bit rushed, they will already feel like they received terrible service. Even if they don't say anything. I hate when someone is late. If I go somewhere, I arrived on time and expect the same from others. I had to fire an attorney because he made me wait so long in the conference room every time I visited. Of course, I understand everyone has issues but everyone has the same amount of time in a given day, so stop wasting mine. Before I fired this attorney, I even had the talk with him, telling him that if he needed an extra 15 or 20 minutes to please let me know so that I could come a little bit later. All I wanted was for him to be as respectful of my time as I was of his time. He was an amazing attorney but he was horrible with time management, so I had to leave him because I simply can't put up with that. And your clients won't put up with that either, especially if you train clients whose time is worth more than $500 per hour and bills by the minute. See how long that client will stay around.

On time is most important for us, especially for the consolation session. To prepare for the consultation, your trainer should be waiting with water, coffee and tea and with a huge smile and warm welcoming greeting for the client. No one is going to buy anything from a boring trainer.

Remember the important dates and details

After you sign up a new client, make sure to keep every birthday and start date in range for your personal trainers to see at least once a month. We have them on our measurement forms with big red colors. This way we know when we need to give our client a gift on top of all the holidays; we do this for their birthday and the anniversary of their start date at our gym. Every month on the same date, especially for women, you need to measure to keep track on the progress and make adjustments if needed and to hold your client accountable. Women's bodies can fluctuate more because of menstruation so they should definitely measure on same date each month.

You need to acknowledge their successes! For instance, if your client loses a certain amount of body fat or inches or is now able to lift so much more, then you need to celebrate it! Do something fun and crazy that will get people talking (and sharing on social media). For example, at 4U Fitness we give out a signed diploma and an acknowledgment letter that was sent to the President of the United States for acknowledgment. And, of course, this letter never makes it to the president, but it does draw a smile and a laugh, especially when they received it unexpectedly in the mail! They always think it's a bill! So when they open it they laugh and they share it on Facebook and Instagram, where they tag us; they are also excited to show it to their spouses and friends We make people smile while drawing extra attention to our gym – it's a win-win! The next time they come in, we give them a framed diploma stating with their name and date and the acknowledgement that they are an official "Bad Ass" and they can check out the competitive list on our website /iAMBadass.

They love it! Truly, these little things make a huge difference and get your clients raving about you.

We also give out a bottle of wine out of the blue on occasion. Our clients are so shocked that they don't know what to say. When it comes to a gift, always include your company name and their name to make it more personal and to advertise because they will have this wine at home and they will pop it open at a gathering with friends and what friend doesn't want to train with a trainer who gives out free bottles of wine for no reason! So, again, your trainer and brand is the center of attention! Your clients will attract more and more people to you. Make sure to reward them, too! We have had clients refer as many as 10 friends and family members - -and referrals are the best way to get – and keep – new business.

When the client asks why they are receiving a spontaneous bottle of wine, your personal trainer can simply let them know that they appreciate having them as a client. If the client asks how they can repay the favor or what they can do in return, your personal trainer can respond with an ask for a referral: You know how I make my living and I could always help some of your friends who are ready to get in shape and get amazing results like you did. If you have some friends interested in better health and fitness, I would love to contact them. Sure enough, they will give you some contact names and phone numbers to call! And, even better, they will let them know that you will call and more than likely these people already know about your trainers since their friend is looking and feeling so great and talking about it.

Reflect back with your clients

You have to teach your trainers that they should pay attention to the client's job title, as well as the word choices they make. Pay close attention to the words and phrases clients' use and reflect their words back. If someone is in the military and you the words like recruit, together as a team, attack and more, your trainer should relate to that and start saying things like "let's recruit those muscles for this exercise," or "let's attack that fat." "You can do this, we can do this together as a team." You get the picture, right? The same thing goes for mothers. But your words change to love, nurture, family, home and much more. Just listen to the words and use them to help your clients relate even more to you. They tell their friends and family members that their personal trainer really gets them and those people will pay attention, too.

Be very careful! If the client runs through the door angry, mad or sad, which is never good news. Do not touch them at this time; your personal trainers should not put an arm around someone who is visibly upset or even shake their hand. Instead, get to work! And during the workout, keep asking how they feel and remind them that they will feel better soon. When they finally tell you or show you how much better they feel (because exercising always makes us feel better), then you can hug them or shake their hands!

Again and again, it comes back to the little things. If you were to make contact with your client right away when he or she is in a terrible mood, they will subconsciously link your training session with feeling upset; however, if you wait until they are feeling better, they will be more open to a high five or hug and they will remember that positive connection instead.! You have to be their happy place, not the other way around These little things are the things that will make a difference and separate your studio from the others in terms of retention. We retain 82% of our clients for more than two years and retain 61% of our clients for more than five years. And most of the people who have left have done so because of divorce, moving away, illness or job loss – not because they actually wanted to leave the studio. That includes our free trials as well and you can imagine that we get quite of a few people who just comes in for the freebie. That happens, but if someone quits over the cost, then you have not provided enough of a value for them to justify the expense.

Think out of the ordinary for your clients. Surprise them with their favorite coffee in the morning. We have an amazing trainer who had a client who really hated to work out so she always canceled at the last minute. However, she did have amazing results! Our wonderful trainer texted every morning to the client when she was supposed to come in with a picture of her favorite coffee, not just a cup of coffee but her absolute favorite, special made coffee for her. This was his way of getting his client going in the morning and giving her a clear path to reach her goal; she just needed the right motivation. So every time they had a session on the schedule, he sent a picture of the coffee, folded hand towels, a smiley face and note that read "we are waiting for you". And each time he changed that note to something different, motivational and funny. Guess what? It worked! She lost more than 60 pounds with us and keeps coming back. And she looks amazing. That was more than a year ago, she is still very happy, looks great and has referred to us seven new clients.

Our clients are all required to sit down with our trainers and go over their goals. So far nothing special, right? Wrong. We sit down with them ask the right questions and pull out the information that we need to know and find out the real reason behind their visit. Everyone says the same thing, but everyone has a real reason behind it! They all say "I want to lose weight." Okay, but why? "So I can be happy." What do you mean by that? And why do you think you will be happy? What would it really feel like for you to reach your goal? I want to know your exact goal! How many pounds do you want to lose and over what period of time, and I want to know the specific reason why! The reasons are all different. Sometimes for a revenge body, sometimes to able to play with kids, get better at sports and more. Really make your clients picture what it would feel like when they reach their goals and describe all the details and specifics.

Than we fill out our client journal together with them accordingly. We put down the goals, dates, training frequency and work out the program, including their grocery list and customized macronutrients specifically calculated for their personal goals. We sit down and create a life plan with the actions they will take to be successful – this is just like you would sit down with a business coach to come up with your business plan. We get into a variety of important details and we keep them accountable for everything That is a must! Keep them accountable!

Always be up front with your clients about their progress, results and work ethic, but never beat them down. Motivate and coach them to be better and never cancel a booked appointment.

If you have a booked appointment, you do not cancel it! Never! Let me be a little more clear: NEVER! I don't care what is going on, you and your personal trainers should never cancel a booked session. It is the worst thing you can do to a client. Yes, I know they cancel every once in a while and some clients cancel most of the time, but that does not give you the right to do the same. This is even worse than showing up late. And as we discussed earlier, showing up late is really bad. It will show them how bad your work ethic is and that you and your staff are not accountable. If you and your personal trainers are not accountable, then how are you going to hold your clients accountable? Do not let your trainers cancel clients. Ever! Unless it was a car accident or something life threatening, your trainer should never cancel the day of the session; if that happens, tell them thank you for your service but please do not come back again. Don't let that be a part of the culture at your gym.

In addition, your personal trainers need to be unique and funny because they are the face of your business. They need to able to maintain, educate and entertain your clients and, most importantly, help to deliver the results that your clients have come to expect.

Make sure they do not blame you, your machine or your trainers if they don't get the results. It is impossible that your clients won't get the results they want if your trainers do all the above things and you have an amazing program for each individual client. You do not want a client who is not happy with you! Why do you think we have only 5 star ratings and hundreds of them? We tell clients up front if we can help them or not; it is important to set this expectation. If they don't fit into our criteria, we just cannot help them.

Your trainers have to teach the clients how it really works and how much work is required to get fit and stay fit. They need to do their homework as well. Your trainers are already doing everything they possibly can, so your clients need to know that they have equal responsibility, if not more! As long as they know that they are responsible for their actions, you are in good shape. Otherwise, you will have a bunch of unsatisfied clients who didn't get what they expected, so they now blame you and your trainers. Here is the thing: If they know how it works and your trainer did an amazing job teaching them, your clients will get the results they desire because they won't want to disappoint you and your trainers. Your trainer needs to be on top of each and every client. If a client says that, "I do not want to do this workout and I do not want to eat healthy, I want to just eat fast food," then your trainers will have to tell them than they are wasting their time and money and can't help them. They need to take the right steps as well. When they go to the doctor and the doctor say take two pills a day, they won't tell the doctor that they only will take half a pill instead. There is a reason behind it and they need to understand that reason. Do not let the clients get off track and get on some magazine crash diet that they just read about where they will surely lose 20 pounds in a month. Your trainers need to educate them and teach them how those crash diets really work. It is very dangerous to have your clients try all these crazy things.

This is a lot to juggle and a lot to keep in mind, but put together, it will ensure that you have a successful seven-figure gym with happy employees and happy clients. Keep your trainers happy and motivated so they can do the same with your clients – a happy trainer will make your clients happy! Show your appreciation to the trainers and clients and let them know that you truly care about them. Without them you wouldn't be in business so you'd better care about their happiness and success. Reward and appreciate them while you hold the clients and trainers equally accountable.

Finally, I suggest that you ask the following three questions to your clients and trainers at least once a year:

1. What do you think we should *start* doing?
2. What do you think we should *stop* doing?
3. What do you think we should *keep* doing?

(I know I read this list of questions from some other amazing book, but I honestly can't remember which one! Apologies and kudos to the author.)

CHAPTER 19:

PUTTING IT ALL TOGETHER

"vision without action is a daydream. Action without vision is a nightmare."

Japanese proverb

Once you have realized that your gym's main purpose is to serve your life and not the other way around, then you can truly take ownership of your business. You will start to make some headway and see real results in terms of your profits as well as client and personal trainer retention. Then and only then, you will finally understand your real purpose and what it really means to work ON your business instead of working IN the business!

While I was writing this book, I was out completely from my studios for three weeks. My employees could reach me through email and text but that was it. They were all reaching their goals that we set from a day to day and week to week perspective and on and on. They all reported their results and they all analyzed what they did right or wrong and were able to adjust and improve. If for some reason they get stuck during this process, I aws always available to listen to them and see how I could help them. Most of the time, they just needed to talk and needed a little motivation. Your trainers are amazing, you just need to make sure you work with them and appreciate them the right way. My business was fully capable of working and even able to grow while I was absent! Yours should be too – it's all about culture, accountability and teamwork.

Analyze and then analyze some more

As a new gym owner, I highly recommend that you analyze your business first. Start with who is doing what and analyze the roles. Even if it's just you at this point, you can still do this. Create a list and on that list, you need to write every single job title that you or someone else is currently doing or should be doing at the moment.

It could look something like this:

Personal Trainer, Receptionist, Customer Service, Social Media Expert, Advertising and Print manager, Website developer, janitor, maintenance, Sales leader, Manager, Human resources manager, Accountant, CEO, COO, CFO and more – depending on your business and your location, you may think up different roles for your gym's current or future needs. Put a name next to each individual role. Then write down exactly what these roles stand for, what this person should be doing day to day in order to make the company move forward. If you have written your name down over and over, you can see where you are heading, right? It is impossible to maintain that in the long run! How do you have time to do all this? You need to make a plan for what can you delegate and when you can do so.

Once you have that plan of delegation, then you will start to see your business grow. Now, I am not saying you need to hire 20 people right now. That would be really stupid. You need to analyze the rules, hire people for them (letting them know that, at the beginning, they will be required to do some additional work) and hold them accountable for each role.

All the while, you need to focus on your job, which is moving your business forward. You are the captain so don't forget to steer the boat while you hire the right people to run the engine for you and take care of the customers on board. Everyone should have their own role and responsibility that they are fully accountable for.

Even if you have 10 roles at the same time, you have to hold yourself accountable for those roles and the jobs need to be completed. Training should not be one of them because that won't help you move forward at all. It is a very time-consuming job – although a very important one. However, you chose to be a business owner, not a personal trainer! As soon as you started your own gym, you chose to step away from making a living as a trainer and got into the business side. At the end of the book, you will see a list of additional recommended reading to help you with this transition.

As a personal trainer, your only responsibility was to provide an amazing service full time and get paid for it. You can make really good money and be happy and have a life with vacation time and benefits as a full-time employee. However, when you are a business owner, all these new things will open up that you have never faced before and if you don't take care of them and scale up, you are going to be enslaved in your business and never get out!

Before you even think about going solo and stop working as a personal trainer, you need to think about it for a minute. Ask yourself why you should start on your own. Are you a business expert? Do you have a business degree? Because a personal training certificate is not enough for running your own gym, unless you have read many books on how to run your own business and you have some good mentors who will help you through it. However, if you are a trainer doing great at a gym and your clients are telling you that you should start you own company because you are amazing but you have no business degree or business knowledge whatsoever, what in the world makes you think you will be able to pull it off? Do you understand what I am asking? For example:

You are a personal trainer and you are amazing at training people, great! So why do you want to quit training people and start your own company your own gym? It is kind of like an airline pilot who is an amazing captain and his passengers and flight attendees tell him that he should start his own airline and that they will follow him there. So he does. What do you think? Do you think a captain of an airline is capable of starting and running his own airplane business if he has no idea how the business really works? All he knows is one part of it, which is flying the plane. As soon as he becomes a business owner, he cannot fly planes anymore. Who will be dealing with employees, sales, marketing, and all the people who are reporting to him, and on top of that how are they going to scale up? He will have hundreds or even thousands of employees to deal with among many other things, and he will probably get very, very overwhelmed and frustrated. His airline will probably go out of business quickly. As a gym owner, you won't be a personal trainer—those positions will be filled by one of your new employees. You are a business owner now you have one thing to focus on. Scaling up your business. If you now understand how it really works, you can continue working on your business plan! Yes, you need one! That is your first step before you even start to think about spaces and prices. You need a full detailed business plan.

Without a plan, you have no chance whatsoever! A goal without a plan is just a dream.

Are you "Home Alone?"

Have you seen the movie "Home Alone" where the family leaves their small child home alone (accidentally) and robbers try to break in? Do you know why this small boy was so successful at protecting the house (other than the fact that anything can happen in the movies)? It's because he had a detailed plan of actions he needed to take. If you don't believe me, watch the movie again and you will see that, before he starts to prep the house, he creates a detailed plan, so all he has to do is follow it and then check back on it time to time to make sure he didn't miss anything and then he can move forward as planned! He had a detailed plan with a timeline he followed the plan and he knew that task 1 has to happen in order to get to task 2 and then 3 and so on. In your business as well, everything has to happen at the right time and in the right order. And you may say he got lucky when he slipped away because he was able to grab the spider that was hanging around the stairs. The thing is that, yes, you will need some luck too, but the harder you work, the luckier you will get! You can't just work and hope for luck. You need a plan of action.

If a kid can do it, then you have absolutely no excuses whatsoever. Your business is like a living organism and you need to have a plan for it. Some people tell me that the plan is in their head – if that's the case, then start putting it on paper – everyone has to start somewhere!

Then once you have a plan, you need to work it! Just because you wrote a plan on paper or created a fancy document on your laptop, you can't just expect it to work for you all of a sudden; just like in the movies, you will have to work your plan in order to make it work!

That doesn't mean that it will be easy and that you won't have some bad things happen along the way. You may start to think that you have bad luck. But on your way, you will meet many great people, employees, mentors and others who will be there for you for the good and the bad, so you can count on them because you have been there for them as well. Even when things are challenging, you need to continue moving forward and to work your plan. Don't give up on yourself!

If you need some help getting started or getting motivated, I recommend checking out this great online one page business plan by Patrick Bet-David at http://www.patrickbetdavid.com/the-one-page-business-plan/

This can help you get started or unstuck when it comes to your business plan. Start with you Big Hairy Audacious Goal and build everything around it – create your ultimate goal and your business plan should be broken down into years, quarters and months with really specific details on how to achieve all of your goals. Start with the basics – any plan is better than no plan and you must start somewhere.

Is a franchise right for you?

According to research, more than 80% of new business, including gyms and personal training studios, will fail in the first five years compared to the franchise business model where only 5% of new businesses fail[12]. That is a huge difference! And do you know why? It is because the franchises all have a working system in place. They are not winging it. A franchise is not just about the brand recognition and a big box name, especially at the beginning when a new franchise starts out. It is all about the working system that comes with it for the franchisee and not about the brand name, recognition or the service or product they are selling. It is all about the HOW. Once again, it comes back to the system.

If you do not have any experience in owning your own business or you don't have a working system and don't know where and how to get it, opening a franchise might be the best option for you.

We came up with our franchise to make a difference in this world and to help many entrepreneurs do what they love to do. We now have a successful full turnkey business for them to take over and succeed with.

Every new business owner receives instructions on how to do things

---

1 Wagner, E. T. (2013, September 12). Five reasons 8 out of 10 businesses fail. For-bes. Retrieved from http://www.forbes.com/sites/ericwagner/2013/09/12/five-rea-sons-8-out-of-10-businesses-fail/#262e66995e3c

2 K, M. (2017). Research on small businesses - start-ups, statistics, SBA, bankruptcy, GEM, failure, business closures, developing countries. Retrieved January 27, 2017, from http://www.moyak.com/papers/small-business-statistics.html

that they might not know, and answers to all of their questions and information on the things they may have never done before. We believe that we came up with the most amazing system out there and you will see many more coming out soon. We spent more than five years perfecting this just to make sure we got the best possible system in place! At the moment, we only offer franchising in the state of Florida but you may see us in other states in the future.

If you are still working IN your business instead of ON your business, if you want to enjoy more vacation time, make money and are interested in owning more than one – maybe up to 10 locations, then franchising is definitely for you! You can build your own empire with us. We just took the heavy lifting out for you. We thought of every single detail and we always focus on improvements as we open new locations and grow. We love to hear from our clients and franchises. We want everyone to know that their opinion is heard and changes are made to make sure we deliver the best service for clients.

The franchise is the prototype that works and it will satisfy your clients, the personal trainers, the managers and of course, the owner!

If you would like to continue learning more about our franchise in particular, the next section is all about our model and our business.

What is 4U Fitness?

4U Fitness is the first and only full-body E-Fit Electric Muscle Stimulation franchise in the United States. We are a high-tech fitness studio with a revolutionary fitness device that uses electrical muscle stimulation to scientifically customize programs and workouts that better fit the needs and goals of each individual.

A busy schedule is no longer an excuse because it only takes two, 20-minute sessions per week to get results! If you can make time to watch a 2-hour movie at the cinema just once or twice a month, then just think about how that same amount of time can get you into lifelong and sustainable shape! You can try us out for free at any one of our locations! And if you sign up for a program, we guarantee results or you will get your money back!

4U Fitness believes in providing the knowledge and tools necessary for clients to lead a permanent healthy lifestyle. We believe that it takes extraordinary efforts to educate those who have been blinded by cookie cutter, "quick-fix" diet and workout programs. With science-based and custom programs, clients are truly successful in fulfilling their goals and desires.

Can people purchase and operate their own studio? Yes, they can! 4U Fitness officially became a franchise as of March 2016. But this company has been operational since 2012. We have spent many years developing and implementing the best all-inclusive program prior to advancing into a franchise business! We receive about five inquiries per week about our franchise and we have yet to spend any money on advertising. We are currently setting up our headquarters and we plan on officially announcing more details on franchising with 4U Fitness in the near future. We are immensely grateful to have so much interest so early in the game; these people truly believe in our brand and our mission.

What comes with the purchase of a franchise?

Just about anything and everything you can ask for! 4U Fitness is the most unique fitness concept in the world with our own line of equipment, supplements and clothing.

We offer unique and beautifully designed studios and we pride ourselves in having developed our own 4U Fitness Academy System for personal trainers. When a trainer applies for a position at 4U Fitness, they are required to partake in a lengthy and thorough interview process. This process entails up to three interviews as well as a personal 1,000-word essay on why they believe we should hire them, what separates them from the other hundreds of applicants that inquire, and how they see themselves working within the company.

After an applicant is chosen they dive into an intense three-month training program before they are allowed to train any one of our clients. Once they pass the program, they will receive a diploma and certification that is required for renewal each year. Since we intend to stay ahead of the game, we want to ensure that our trainers are always up-to-date with our programs.

In summary, here is what a purchaser will receive in a 4U Fitness franchise:

- Supplement and equipment line
- Academy System
- Assistance with real estate
- Construction and design
- Technology
- Full Guide and Support for Hiring
- Operations Manual and Support
- Sales Process
- Website and warranty
- Grand opening party
- Marketing plan
- Documents and waiver
- Quality checks
- Spokesmodels
- ...and much more.

Let's put it this way. We believe that we are the Apple and Tesla of the fitness industry. We have a detailed 10-year business plan including all goals and product launch dates. Stay tuned for our master plan.

We have created a demand for our services and have been given some amazing opportunities to continue our growth. Most recently, we were flown to Los Angeles to appear as guests on a famous TV show "The Doctors." We were asked to demonstrate and provide more information about our specialized program to a nationwide and global audience. In 2016, we also visited Europe to meet with our supplement and equipment manufacturer personally. We constructed and viewed our products first-hand. All of this helps to create our culture of accountability.

What does 4U Fitness stand for and what is the mission?

Our ultimate goal is to eliminate the clutter and implement our science-based programs into the minds and lifestyles of individuals. When people think of health and fitness, they will think of us!

Let me give you an example:

If I were to ask you to call me tomorrow, you have a way different picture in mind than your parents did at your age! You are picturing yourself pulling out your smartphone and not a big plastic piece of junk on the wall with a mile of cable hanging out of it.

So, that's our goal! By the time your kids grow up when they think of fitness they won't think of countless hours in the gym combined with crazy cardio and a crash diet. No, they will think of us instead! Just like by the time they grow up they will also picture cars differently! Tesla's goal is the same! By the time the kids grow up, Tesla wants to make sure that when you think of a car you won't think of the inefficient gas or diesel cars but that you will think of electric. That is the picture that comes into your mind. We promise to provide scientifically-based knowledge and programs that will lead you to thinking differently!

At 4U Fitness, we don't need contracts since we have been validated by the return of our clients time and time and time again. Clients stay with us for years because they get their desired results. We then have the ability to provide them with a maintenance and sustainable program that they can practice on their own (besides the EMS). We deliver efficient programs that speak for themselves. We have no need to lock people into ridiculous year-long contracts that normally are drawn up as a cover up for unsuccessful results.

We want to educate everyone on how the system really works. You truly don't have to succumb to the slimy salespeople at commercial gyms. Happiness and health can arise from a balanced change in lifestyle. With the proper implementation of a workout routine and healthy food choices, we as a nation can fight the obesity epidemic in the United States. One person dies from obesity every 90 seconds. This rate will continue to climb if we do not put a stop to it.

We firmly believe that we can help combat this epidemic by providing the appropriate education on how to create and maintain a healthy lifestyle. It's time to think differently and 4U Fitness is here to implement actual, achievable and maintainable results.

CHAPTER 20: ——————————

FEED YOUR BRAIN

"A mind always employed is always happy."

Thomas Jefferson

If you want to be a seven-figure gym owner, you have to switch gears. It used to be all about your looks and about your muscles and working out so much. To be successful today, you have to switch gears and do the same but with your brain. To earn the title of successful business owner and CEO, you must feed your brain. Just like your muscles get stronger from working out, your brain gets stronger when you exercise it. Feed your brain regularly. Yes, this means healthy nutrition but it also means reading, reading and reading some more. I personally read an absolute minimum of four books per month, not magazines. Your fitness magazine subscriptions will not teach you how to run a successful personal training studio or gym.

When I first started out as a personal trainer, I woke up at 4:45 a.m. every morning to work out. As a personal trainer, I knew that I had to look the part. Now that has changed. I still look the part, don't get me wrong, being fit and healthy should be a top priority for everyone. But now I get up at the same time every day except for Sunday and I read for the first two hours of the day. No matter what! Just like you schedule a time to work out and you never miss it, I schedule time to feed my brain. You should block of a time for reading and learning; if you sleep more than six or seven hours a night, you might be able to cut back on sleep or social media time to make time for your brain.

"The Chicago Tribune" interviewed me about how to make your first million the Warren Buffet way (if you want to read the full article, simply Google "Daniel Nyiri and Warren Buffet" and it will pop up right away). And what did I tell them? I talked a lot about reading and learning. You do not need a college degree to become a millionaire! And you don't have to come from a wealthy family either. You can create wealth for yourself. But if you don't learn how to create it and then how to manage it, you will never have what you desire. It all comes back to reading and learning again and again. Warren Buffet, who is one of the richest and most successful people on earth, reportedly reads four hours a day. My schedule is to get up every morning at 4:45 a.m., take a shower, go over my goals in my head, read my notebook so I am up-to-date on everything, and then from 5:05 a.m., I am reading till 7 a.m. That is my morning ritual.

No matter what else is going on, I organize my day around reading. You, however, might think that you don't time for that. You might say, "I work out at that time or have clients". No, you don't have time because you are unwilling to make time for learning. Arnold Schwarzenegger, who is also pretty fit and healthy, has said that you only need about six hours of sleep each night. So you still have time to work, eat, workout and learn and recreate yourself. Read. Everyone has the same amount of time in life so use it wisely! When you make it part of your daily schedule, it will become an enjoyable ritual each day.

People ask me how I have the time to read so much.

First of all, this is no secret... finding time to read comes down to choice.

Always continue learning! I find it astonishing to meet other business owners who tell me what they don't read books. And there is always an excuse like "I don't have time" or" I am just too busy." I believe there are two things wrong with those statements. Number one, they are probably spending most of their time working in the business instead of on the business, making it easy for them to think they have no free time. Number two comes down to choice. When I happen to ask these people about any current hit TV show, they can describe every character and want to discuss the latest episode. I end up offering my apologies to them because I do not watch TV. However, I could recommend a vast number of great business books that could solve the problems they are currently facing. And when I offer this advice, instead of saying "oh man, thank you let me write that title down," they generally ignore this tip. Keep in mind that these are the people who will start making up stories about you when you've made it and your dreams come true. They will say things like: he got lucky, his family is rich, he married rich, he is not happy, he will burn out, it is in his genetics, he has a photogenic memory, it's easy for him or whatever it is. Again, they just don't see the hustle you go through every day, the hard work and what it actually takes! All they see is the finished product. Now think for a second -- isn't this the same thing that many overweight people say when they see a fit person? They say things like oh he is young, when he gets my age, or its genetics. They are also mistaken and they are usually making excuses.

As I mentioned, I don't really watch TV. And I would not be able to name any of your favorite characters on TV and no, I do not watch "The Walking Dead" or "The Kardashians" or whatever is currently hot. I only know about them because everyone talks about these shows, especially the ones who should not talk about watching so much TV. They should invest in themselves to be able to move up in life. Sometimes, my TV is on in the background but I'm not paying attention to it. I just like a little background noise. For some reason, this background noise helps my concentration, but this won't work for everyone; if you get distracted by the TV, turn it off and try some classical music instead.

An average person sleeps for eight or nine hours a day and spends another three or four hours watching TV, one hour or more commuting and another two or three hours a week shopping. That's about 25 hours per week, without counting the sleep hours and it equals 1,500 minutes. If you read a page a minute, that should be 1,500 pages a week.

Of course, the same goes for exercise! We developed our system for people who keep saying they don't have time to work out!

Most people spend countless hours per week in the gym! And yet they don't have time to read. That's hard to believe. If you want to be a CEO of your fitness empire one day, then you must be prepared to be paid to use your brain. That means that it's in your best interest to grow that brain as big as possible!

For example, take a look at Arnold Schwarzenegger – first, he was in the fitness industry and had to build muscle in order to succeed in his field. So he worked hard and spent countless hours to make his muscles the biggest in order to become Mr. Olympia multiple times, and on top of that, he also chose to feed his brain and became very successful in business as well. As you may know, he came from nothing, but he was dedicated to going after his dreams. It had nothing to do with luck. He worked his butt off. Reading, working, studying, networking, every day!

Reading isn't something to be done once a week and to check off your list, it's something that needs to be done every day.

Why do I read? I read so I can stay on top of my game. This information is out there for everyone, and if my competition is not reading, I am already ahead of them. But I mainly read to increase my knowledge and to improve my English.

Warren Buffet once said that the rich invest in time, the poor invest in money. I totally agree with that.

All of the entrepreneurs who fail in their business, 85% of them have one major thing in common: they only read from one to five books per year[1]. Of those who come from nothing to become millionaires, there is another important statistic that they share: they read a minimum of four books per month.

Lastly, just ask yourself these questions: How do I benefit from watching TV or listening to the radio? Or how does my business benefit from these things? Because if your goal is to make it big and get ahead of the competition, then you better get to reading and acquiring new information though business coaches and mentors.

I have business coaches and mentors as well. They are a very important part of my life, and I highly recommend taking the time to find the right ones for you. I am even available for mentoring, but my time is very limited because I only take on a few people to mentor so I can really commit to their success. As a mentor, I first analyze my mentee's business and explain how I might be able to help. I always try to find solutions to issues and challenges.

If you are planning to reach out to a business coach or mentor, do not wait till the last second. You need to plan ahead. Reach out when you feel like you've got it. Most people make the mistake of reaching out when everything is already close to lost.

If you are just starting out or if your gym or personal training studio is in trouble, you can hire me for coaching. Here is the best part: You can take our FITBIZ test on our website for free. I will review your score and I will give you my honest opinion, then you can decide if you would like to hire me or not. On my personal website you can also find out where I am at any time because I speak at events and my schedule for the next three events is usually up there.

You can also send me an email to inquire about a visit to your studio for public speaking or even working with your team to increase

---

1 Merle, A. (2016, April 14). The reading habits of ultra-successful people. Huffington Post. Retrieved from http://www.huffingtonpost.com/andrew-merle/the-reading-habits-of-ult_b_9688130.html

effectiveness. I'd also be happy to help you fix any issue you may facing in your business, so please don't hesitate to email me at DanielNyiri@4u-fitness.com

If your gym is failing, and you want my help, I will take you as a client only because I believe it's still fixable. You don't even have to pay me until I have fixed your company. We can use those funds instead to help to rebuild your company and once that investment was worth it, you can pay me back.

Then we would come up with your core values as a business. This step is very important especially if you plan on growing you company. After we established your core values we would figure out your WHY. Why are you in business? Why are you unique? What problem are you solving? What is your sole purpose?

Here is a link to my article in the Chicago Tribune:

Chicago Tribune Article - How to Make Your First Million the Warren Buffet Way

http://www.chicagotribune.com/business/ct-personal-finance-warren-buffett-20161013-story.html

CONCLUSION: ————————————————————

Don't start a company unless it's an obsession or something that you truly love. If you have an exit plan, it's not a company that you truly love and that will succeed.

Time is more valuable than money so don't try to do everything yourself. Yes, at the very beginning you will have to do everything when you have no money. But no, you don't need a lot of money to start a business. Numerous companies, including ours, started with nothing. Once you acquire money, make sure to utilize it appropriately. Know your value and don't try to fix the broken computer, toilet, AC or whatever else needs fixing thinking that you can do it all. I used to do that. I even bought tools for my AC unit to fix it myself. I spent hours working on it and once it was fixed I was so proud I did it. And then I realized I wasted so many hours. The AC guy could have fixed it in less than two hours for $150 and it took me half a day. At that time my value per hour was $150 per hour, so I wasted about $800. Lesson learned.

If you really like what you do, you should and will never give up! If you don't like what you are doing, remember that life is too short: find something that you truly love and believe in it. If you like what you are doing, it is no longer work. I wake up every day and I look forward to each day! To me my job is not work, rather it's a challenge I face every day and I look forward to it – I can't wait for the day to begin. It is an amazing adventure and, most importantly, I get to do amazing things with amazing people: helping others get great results while creating good paying jobs!

Yes, you will have to face many risks along the way. But that is part of running a business and part of being alive. Do something important.

Scare yourself a little. Try something new. When you work hard and surround yourself with the best people, you will be able to handle the challenges that arise. Just like sports, there are always challenges in business. If you can't overcome daily hardships, then being an entrepreneur might not be for you.

Create a company that will make a lasting impact in the world – that is exactly what I want for 4U FITNESS!

BONUS INTERVIEW: ————————————

Dr. Jacob Wilson, CEO and Ryan Lowery, President at Applied Science and Performance Institute (ASPI)

Facebook: @ASPITraining Twitter: @themusclephd Instagram: @themusclephd

Dr. Jacon Wilson and Ryan Lowery have published more than 150 papers, book chapters and abstracts on muscle, supplementation, sports nutrition and resistance training for bodybuilders and strength athletes. They have covered both the cellular and molecular responses to supplementation and nutrition, as well as the whole body changes in muscle size, strength, and power. Information from: *bodybuilding.com*

1) What do you spend most of your time on nowadays? What is your big vision?

Our mission at ASPI is to change lives through science and innovation. Our vision is to help inspire anyone from your elite athlete to youth to the average person to optimize their lives through fitness, nutrition and supplementation. We are planning to expand to include ASPI medical, a medical division to help further build upon our services.

2) How big is your facility and how many Employees/Students/ Interns do you have?

ASPI is 22,000 square feet with more than 25 scientists, coache, and research assistants.

3) Do you have a niche market and how did you decide on the one you wanted to go after?

We tend to work more with elite and professional youth and elite athletes, but work with all ranges to study the limits of human performance.

4) Do you use any form of advertisement? (social media, Google, etc.)

We have built an extensive social media following over the past several years and, through various platforms, have several million followers. The best form of advertisement, however, is word of mouth. If people have great experiences at the facility it is that word of mouth awareness that truly helps the company build.

5) Any advice you want to give for others looking to start a business?

Find what you are passionate about and never stop striving to achieve that. Find something worth fighting for and go after it. When you are passionate about something it shows and those who are passionate are the ones who change the world.

BONUS INTERVIEW: ———————

Mike Arce CEO of Loud Rumor

Loudrumor.com
Twitter: @Mike_J_Arce
Facebook: @boom.loudrumor

How long have you been in business and how would you describe your business in a few sentences?

I founded Loud Rumor in November 2009. We are a lead-generation company for fitness studios and independent gyms supported by sales and marketing training.

How many gyms do you currently work with?

As of January 2017, we're working with over 100 fitness studios and independent gyms throughout the world.

How important is a great system?

When it comes to business, if you're looking to build a company that can run and grow without you and scale, having great systems and processes in place is not an option. Too many business owners have a business that depends on them and/or a few key employees and who seem to store all their "systems and processes" in their heads. Everything needs to be documented. This allows you to grow your company regardless of personnel changes, because people shouldn't run a company. Great systems should run a company and great people should run the systems.

How do you attract the right customer?

In order to attract the right customer, you first have to know who the right customer is. If you were a fisherman and you wanted to catch salmon, you don't go fishing where salmon don't swim. You'd be most successful fishing where there are tons of salmon. That being said, identifying the traits and characteristics of your ideal customer is extremely important. The best way to start this is by looking at your entire customer base and separating your favorite customers from everyone else. Once you've done that, you'll want to look for the common characteristics for all of those customers. You'll want to look at things like age, gender, how they heard about you, goals, personality, work ethic, commitment, hobbies, and what they spend most of their time doing. Once you've identified what they all have in common, you'll then want to create a customer persona.

This basically sums up your ideal customer. Next, you'll want to learn where this ideal customer spends most of their time and how they buy. In a general statement, fitness studios and gyms get the most value when targeting men and women between 25-55 years old who have a goal to lose fat and strengthen muscle. However, you will find out specifically what your ideal customer is like. Some gyms target competitors who want to be on stage and win physique competitions. Others target new moms who want to burn off the baby fat. There are so many other types of people to target. Going strictly off age, Facebook advertising has been across the board a fantastic platform to generate leads in the fitness industry. However, when creating your ads and landing pages that you'll send people to, you'll use your buyer persona to determine the ad copy and design that they'll see in order to be very clear on what you do, how you do it, and why you do it. If all is done correctly, the right customers will bite.

Why is it important to know your niche market instead of marketing to everyone?

Knowing your niche market makes life a lot easier. You know exactly what to build content around such as videos, blogs, social media posts, seminars, etc. For instance, if your niche is new moms who want to lose the baby fat, all your content will strictly be content that those in your niche would find valuable. This means you can skip building general content such "How to Pack on Muscle" or "Get in Wedding Shape." You can create content that's interesting to o the average person that's in your niche such as "How to Get Your Child to Eat More Protein" or "Healthy Meals that Moms and Kids Both Love." Niching also allows your employees to really get great at helping that ONE type of person and get educated faster. Your customers typically get better service and are usually willing to pay more for it. If I wanted to be a better hockey goalie, I'd much rather pay a personal trainer who specifically trains hockey goalies exclusively versus a personal trainer who helps anybody with anything. I'd even be willing to pay him more! And his content is most likely much more valuable to me since all he talks about are ways to specifically help people like me. Referrals are much more common (although most that are afraid to niche can't believe it), and upgrades and upsells are far easier as your buyer trusts that the product exists to help people with their exact goal!

Do you take on new gyms if they don't know who is their market (if they say everyone is their market)?

We most enjoy working with fitness studios and gyms that have a clear understanding as to who their target market is. However, sometimes they're not as clear on this as they should be. After doing this for so long, we can often identify their ideal target market because our fitness studios and gyms are simply based on the style of service, location, brand message, and current customer base. Anybody that says "Everyone is in my target market" hasn't spent time doing their research and is destined to always work harder than they have to in order to grow their business.

Do you have a niche market?

I absolutely have a niche market. I didn't for a while and was extremely scared to niche even though many strongly suggested it to me. For seven years I owned a digital marketing agency that helped any small business. If you were a dentist, chiropractor, personal trainer, catering company, or birthday clown (seriously), we'd take you on as a client. In those seven years I couldn't break $500,000 in annual revenue and my margins were terrible because creating a smooth system for so many different types of people and goals wasn't easy. In March 2017, we niched and began exclusively working with fitness studios and we hit $1,018,000 in that very first year! On top of that, we tripled our clientele and because our system was so smooth we were able to charge 33% less than we were before (which makes it easier for more clients to afford you), yet increase profit margins by more than triple! The riches are in the niches and I never believed it more than I do now. Since niching I've convinced four other friends in the fitness space to do the same and their business has skyrocketed, but more importantly... they're happier, less stressed, and have a much clearer vision of their future, like me.

If you want to grow your brand and have people talk about you and know who you are, you need to get your name out there. One of the easiest ways to do so is having your pitch down really well and going to social events where you meet other business professionals. But I highly recommend you try to find networking events where your client would hang out; you will be more likely to attract new clients this way.

If you are at a business event, then your focus should be mainly on building your brand. Of course, you need to do this. There is nothing better than when a highly successful businessperson who has become your client starts to introduce you to his/her peers. There is nothing more valuable than that. They are instantly sold! This is why the golden rule is that you never turn down an invitation from your client. They will be so happy to invite you out and introduce you to all of their friends. Any time we went to an event like that, we walked away with three to five new clients. And those clients stay forever and ever unless you mess something up.

Look on your local Chamber of Commerce's website for new business openings, and then go out there and introduce yourself to the new business owner. You can give him or her a deal and say that all of their new customers will receive a free session or whatever you deal or promotion you decide to offer. You just have to make sure it's free, without a catch and has a deadline (for instance, they need to come in in the next seven days or they lose it) and it should definitely have some real value. Ask some of your clients to go check out this new business, and, in return, you can give them a free session. Make sure you tell these clients to mention your business and that you sent them over. This is a great way to set up a new connection and it can pay off now and in the future.

You also did your good deed for the day – helping out a local business and your clients – so that is a win-win in anybody's book.

BONUS INTERVIEW: ————————

ERIN STERN, two-time Ms. Figure Olympia Champion
erinstern.com
Twitter: @erinfast
Facebook: /fiterin

Introduction: I'm a self-coached lifetime natural athlete, a two-time Ms. Figure Olympia Champion, and former Division I Junior All American high jumper. I'm an author, speaker, and I have created several successful online training programs.

What do you spend most of your time on?

I spend a great deal of time creating content and managing social media.

Do you still train clients? If no, why not and if yes, why?

I train a few clients online. I prefer not to train, as it's very time-consuming.

Do you have a niche market and how did you decide on the one you wanted to go after?

Yes. I have a following of women who want to look like they compete (figure), but who don't actually want to get on stage. I built a brand based on empowering, educating, and enriching the lives of people through health and fitness.

Who is the ideal customer?

The ideal customer is between 25-45, female, and wants to live a healthy, fit lifestyle.

Do you use any form of advertisement?

I just use social media and the following I have.

Any advice you want to give for fellow gym owners?

I would think that hiring good managers would be helpful. This would free up time for the owner to focus on getting more business and focus on future plans.

RECOMMENDED READING:————————

Mark Cuban, owner of the Dallas Mavericks, once said that even when he had no money, he would actually spend money on books because he could possibly get at least one good idea from a book that he could use in his business to help him make more money. I hope that you will find at least one if not many useful things in my book that were worth your investment and your time.

Following is a recommended book list for the new CEO or entrepreneur:

The Life of an Entrepreneur in 90 Pages
by Patrick Bet David

This is also one of those books that should be on your reading list. Even though it is only 90 pages, you are provided with information that might prevent you from making huge mistakes in the future and it will give you a general guide on the road ahead.

Doing the Impossible by Patrick Bet-David

An amazing short book with many of my favorite quotes! I really liked the hard work aspect of this book. People want results without the work, and the books that promise that really do people a disservice. Patrick does a great job on emphasizing that fact. You should evaluate your commitment to do the work, and feel motivated to make it happen. I highly recommend this book to anyone who is starting out or already in business!

The Dip by Seth Godin - This book was recommended to me by Topher Morrison.

When I read the first page, I almost threw it out because the first comments mentioned quitting. However, after reading the next couple of pages, I realized the real value of this book. It explains the "dip" and why so many people fail to succeed and fail to quit and how to not become average. If you want to be average, then just quit already. This book is for people who want to be the #1 in their industry and it explains how to take advantage of that spot. This book teaches you how to become the #1 in your area and even in the world. It's a quick read.

Emyth by Michael Gerber

This book will show you exactly how a business is supposed to work and why most people who start a business because they love what they do are good at it actually fail more than 85% of the time.

Bulls-eye by Brian Tracy

This is a great, short book about concentration and goal setting. It also discussed the importance of order and daily planning, it is a system that I use myself with the A, B, C, D system. A is the most important task of the day and you most get it down first so that you can move forward or you will face consequences. B is something you should do; it is a task that needs to be done soon but definitely not before you have completed any of your A tasks. C is things that are nice to do, something easy and pleasant like social media, emails whatever. D is to delegate a task to someone else to free up your time so you can work on tasks that are most important to your career. E is eliminate for the things that you should simply just say no to.

Leadership and the One Minute Manager by Ken Blanchard

This is an amazing book about the situational leadership, which is the most effective leadership. This book will teach you that there is nothing so unequal as the equal treatment of unequals and that every single person you hire has peak performance potential- you just need to know where they are coming from and meet them there.

It is a very quick read of only 100 pages. This book is priceless. Every business owner, entrepreneur or manager who is about to hire or manage people should read this book. And if you already do those things and you haven't read this book before, you are really missing out and you are probably making huge mistakes right now. This will teach you how to take care of your trainers!

The Ultimate Blueprint for an Insanely Successful Business by Keith J. Cunningham

What a great book! I highly recommend this book to anyone in business. If you don't have a CFO, this book should be the first book on your to-do list. If you currently have a CFO, you should still read it unless you have an MBA in accounting. There is no reason not to read this. It will give you all the tools you will need to read the scoreboard of your business. If you can't interpret the score, then how do you know if you are winning or losing? If you are someone who hates numbers, or even worse, you just don't understand them, then I recommend that you buy this book right now. This book will teach you how to measure your success without an MBA and it will show you how to discover the things that are draining your business. Furthermore, it will give you some info on how to fix it as well.

The Happiness Advantage by Shawn Achor

This is one of my favorite books! I wish that I had read this book a long time ago. It was recommended to me by Richard Branson and am happy to recommend it to you now. Your competition will outperform you if they are using the principles from this book, so reading it will up your competitive advantage. It has helped me become a better person, husband and leader. If you know me, you know that I am a very positive person. But this book opened the world of positives for me on a whole new level! Now people benefit even more from my positives. It is full of case studies with useful advice and examples as well.

Think and Grow Rich by Napoleon Hill

This is also one of those books that every entrepreneur should read. To me, this was basic knowledge because I grew up in a situation similar to the story in the book and I was already doing everything that the book described. However, it was really amazing to be reassured about how the system really works.

Smarter Faster Better by Charles Duhigg

This book has lots of useful information on how to be more productive and accomplish more. I liked how the author used real life stories to make his points.

Digital BACON by Alex Rodriguez

The book is amazing. The author has a very successful company and he gives away all his secret formulas in this book. So if you want an edge on advertising or you just want to have a great understanding of it before hiring an expert, this is the book to read.

5 Temptations of a CEO by Patrick Lencioni

This is my top book for the month. I believe every CEO, manager, leader, coach and entrepreneur should read it. In my opinion, this book is key to the success of any business. The information in this book will help you realize the 5 most common temptations. And I can almost guarantee that when you read this, you will find that you have at least one of the five temptations. While I was reading this book, I kept thinking that I wish I had read it many years ago! I would have done so many things differently. Patrick Lencioni does an amazing job delivering the story and connecting the theme to the reader. It is one of those books that you just can't put down once you start reading because you just have to know what's next. Luckily this book is only about 150 pages so you can finish it in a couple hours. I highly recommend it!